The Lower Rappahannock River Fords of Culpeper County

Including the history of Chinquapin Neck and the village of Richardsville

Steven L. Walker

"The Lower Rappahannock River Fords of Culpeper County" by Steven L. Walker. ISBN 978-1-60264-617-9

Published 2010 by Virtualbookworm.com Publishing Inc., P.O. Box 9949, College Station, TX 77842, US. ©2010, Steven L. Walker. All rights reserved. No part of this publication may be reproduced, stored in a retrieval system, or transmitted in any form or by any means, electronic, mechanical, recording or otherwise, without the prior written permission of Steven L. Walker.

Manufactured in the United States of America.

Contents

Acknowledgements		iii
Introduction		1
Chapter One	Richards Ford	3
Chapter Two	Emburys and Bells Ford	18
Chapter Three	Skinkers/ Rocky/ Martins Ford	21
Chapter Four	Ellis Ford	29
Chapter Five	Rogers/ Kempers Ford	49
Epilogue		53
Maps		54
Pictures		60
Appendix I	Rapidan River Fords	70
Appendix II	Mills of Chinquapin Neck	72
Appendix III	Gold Mines	74
Appendix IV	Schools; Stores; Churches; Cemeteries	78
Appendix V	Company E 13th Virginia Infantry	84
Appendix VI	Ambushes and Engagements Chinquapin Neck Fords	96
Appendix VII	Early residents of the Richardsville area	101
Appendix VIII	Postmasters	123
Appendix IX,	GPS/MAP Coordinates	124
BIBLIOGRAPHY		125
INDEX		130

Acknowledgements

To Fred Ricker, the honorary Mayor and most respected resident of Richardsville. This book would have been impossible without his knowledge and help. Also to Mark Whitney, a good friend that help me in every step.

Introduction

East of Culpeper, located on a pleasant country road, is the village of Richardsville. Richardsville is the gateway to the Rappahannock River fords in eastern Culpeper County. Time has been gentle to this little settlement, and it retains much of its original character. The country store, built in the 1880s, is where the first residents congregated, the churches are where they worshiped, the houses are where they lived, and the cemeteries disclose their names. Richardsville is an unpretentious little place where life has remained simple for the past 200 years.

Originally known as Smith's Tavern, the name of the village changed to Richardsville upon getting a post office in the early 1800s, most likely because the postmaster was named William Thomas Jefferson Richards. The Richards actually lived more than five miles away on the Rappahannock River. A more appropriate name may have been Humphreysville. The Humphreys were a prominent local family, and in 1843 John Humphreys built the oldest house still standing in Richardsville. John was also a founding member of Richardsville's Oakland Baptist Church. In the back of the church is his grave, marked with his initials scratched on a simple fieldstone.

The region around Richardsville has been called by several names, including "Great Fork," "Chinquapin Neck," and the "The Neck." "Great Fork" was its earliest designation because it represented where the Rappahannock and the Rapidan Rivers come together. It also distinguished it from the upstream confluence of the Hazel and Rappahannock River, which was called "Little Fork." In the 1800s the name "Chinquapin Neck" became popular because of the once many Chinquapin trees in the area. The Chinquapins are long gone and the name was shortened to "The Neck." Now the region is simply known as Richardsville.

The area is truly a neck of land located between the two rivers. The beginning of the neck, which is its narrowest point, is only two miles wide. From there the land broadens out, then narrows back down at the confluence of the Rappahannock and Rapidan Rivers. Because the rivers limited access to the region, it has always been sparsely populated and the soils are infertile so it has also remained heavily forested.

Within these forests lies a tremendous amount of history. Beginning with the Indians, then the explorers and settlers, through the gold rushes and the Civil War, "The Neck" has it all. The rivers played a major role in the history, and the various fords were at the core of it. These crossings not only facilitated transportation in and out, they became geographic locations that can still be identified. But most important, the fords on the Rappahannock River have a story.

Chapter One

Richards Ford

Indian folklore tells of great powers where rivers come together. If there is a place where there are great powers, it is where the Rappahannock and Rapidan Rivers meet. The rivers merge into a broad set of rapids that flow for over a mile. The rocks and boulders are evenly spaced, and the view is panoramic. It is peaceful and breathtaking at the same time. The setting does indeed make the confluence of these two rivers a spiritual place, and about a mile upstream of this magnificent spot, on the south side of the Rappahannock, was the Indian village of Hassiningua and the location of Richards Ford.

Indians

Originally located on the south side of the ford was the Manahoac Indian village of Hassiningua. The river crossing linked them by trail to the falls on the Rappahannock River at Fredericksburg. In the river next to the village is a long set of rapids. The rapids provided a food source for the Indians because they allowed for fish traps. The traps were rocks in the river, arranged in a V, with a basket or branches at the end of the V. The Indians would drive fish into the V and catch them in the basket or spear them in the confined space.

Manahoacs were of Sioux ancestry and spoke a Siouan language. Their enemies included the Powhatan Confederacy, who spoke Algonkian and lived in the Chesapeake area. Interestingly, one of the tribes belonging to the confederacy was called Rappahnannock and lived further downstream, past Fredericksburg.

There were many Manahoac villages on the Rappahnannock and Rapidan Rivers, but only one of them can be located with any certainty, and that is Hassiningua. It was revealed in the autumn of 1608 when Captain John Smith of Jamestown sailed up the Rappahannock. He was on an expedition that was part of a series of his trips exploring the Chesapeake Bay. Smith's purpose was to find out if there was a passage to the Pacific. He searched every inlet, creek, and river, all the way to present day Baltimore. Along with making maps, Smith carefully documented his contact with the Indians. Fortunately his records include a map and description of the Rappahannock River and the Indians who lived on it.

Smith went up the Rappahannock until he was stopped by a set of rapids, now the location of Fredericksburg. Smith went ashore on the north side of the river, now Falmouth. There he made contact with the local Indians, including those from what is now Richards Ford. Smith had already made contact with several Indian tribes as he came up the river, but they all belonged to the Powhatan Confederacy. These Indians were not Powhatans, they were Manahoacs and they were not friendly. Soon after Smith and his men came ashore, they were attacked.

Smith had inadvertently sailed into an annual Indian hunting-fishing party. The Indians were from various Manahoac tribes along the upper Rappahannock and Rapidan Rivers. While on shore, Smith and his party were attacked by what he claims to be about one hundred Indians. The fight lasted for about thirty minutes and the Indians disappeared as quickly as they appeared. None of Smith's group was injured, but they did manage to shoot an Indian in the knee and capture him. His name was Amoroleck. He was from a tribe called Hassininga whose village was located about seventeen miles up the Rappahannock River, one mile before the confluence with the Rapidan River.

Amoroleck was taken aboard the ship and questioned by Smith's interpreter, an Algonkian Indian from the Potomac named Mosco. Algonkians were enemies of the Manahoacs and Mosco at first tried to attack Amoroleck.[1] Smith writes of the questioning:

> *"Then we desired Mosco to know what he was what Countries were beyond the mountains: the poor savage mildly answered, he and all with him were of Hassininga, where there are three Kings more, like unto them, namely the King of Stegora, the King of Tauxuntania, and the King of Shakahonea, that were come to Mohaskahod, which is only a hunting Towne, and the bounds betwixt the Kingdome of the Mannahocks and the Nandtaughtacunds, but hard by where we were."*[2]

During the interrogation Smith asked why his people attacked. Amoroleck replied, *"they heard we were from the under world, to take their world from them."*[3] Word was out, evidently the Europeans' reputation had proceeded them.

Smith obtained enough information from Amoralack to later make a map of the river. The map identifies the various Indian villages on the Rappahannock and Rapidan Rivers. Mohaskahod was the name of the hunting camp they sailed into. Hassininga, Amoroleck's village, was named after the chief of the village, which also happened to be Amoroleck's brother.

Hassininga and the three other Manahoac chiefs, Stegora, Tauxuntania, and Shakahonea had come to Mohaskahod with their warriors for the annual event. When Smith wandered in, the other chiefs and their warriors were out hunting. Amoroleck told Mosco that they would be returning to camp at dark. Mosco, obviously familiar with the Manahoacs, told Smith that they should leave. Smith agreed, but not until nightfall. Mosco, understanding the situation, did the next best thing. He sharpened his arrows.

After dark, when Smith and his group returned to the ships, they proceeded to sail back down the river, taking Amoraleck with them. It wasn't long before the swishing sound of arrows could be heard coming at the ship. All night long the Indians followed, screaming war cries and shooting arrows. Occasionally Smith's men would shoot back, aiming at where they had heard a yell. At daylight, Smith had come to where he felt the river was wide enough to stop and still be safe. He then dropped the anchor and promptly ate breakfast.

Refreshed, Smith decided to talk with the Indians on shore. He went on deck, made sure his armed men could be seen, and presented his prisoner Amoroleck. Amoroleck and the Indians yelled back and forth to each other until Amoroleck somehow convinced his people that Smith meant no harm. Smith then came ashore with Amoroleck

---

1 David I. Bushnell, Jr., *The Manahoac Tribes In Virginia*, 1608, (City of Washington, Smithsonian Institution, 1936), p. 4.
2 John Smith, *The Generall Historie of Virginia,... in Travels and Works of Captain John Smith*, ed. Edward Arber II (Edinburgh: John Grant, 1910), p. 427: pp. 421-429 covers entire meeting.
3 Ibid., p. 427.

and met with the chiefs. He traded with them, though the Indians had nothing Smith really wanted. The Indians, however, took pistols because they wanted them for pipes. Afterward, Smith sailed away watching 500 merry Indians dancing and waving goodbye.

No other contact has ever been recorded. It is not known what happened to Amoroleck. For a long time, the Powhatan tribes of the lower Rappahannock prevented any further interaction between white settlers and the Manahoacs. By the time explorers came through in 1670, the Manahoacs were gone, most victims of disease, possibly from Smith himself. The rest were displaced by Iroquois and Susquehannock warriors searching for fur. The European demand for fur was a prime example of how world trade could affect local people, even though the people never had any contact with the world.

Some Manahoacs show up near Richmond in 1656. They participated in a battle against the white settlers and their Powhatan allies. The Manahoacs and their allies, the Monacans, won the battle. The Monacans, another tribe of Sioux origin, lived on the upper James River. Fearing reprisal, the Manahoacs left the Richmond area and settled near the James River, twenty-five miles upstream of Richmond, at a place called Mohawk Creek. Mohawk is obviously a white man's later distortion of the name Manahoac. Other Manahoacs are believed to have moved west, over the mountains, to the unpopulated areas of eastern Kentucky's Big Sandy River. In 1669, only fifty Manahoac "bowmen" were reported to live on the frontier between the James and Rappahannock Rivers.[4]

Exploration

There is no other record of the Richards Ford until August 21, 1670. On that day a German physician-explorer named John Lederer crossed the river there. It was his third expedition into the frontier of Virginia. In 1665, the governor of Virginia, William Berkeley, commissioned Lederer to make these journeys. At that time it was believed that an overland route could be found to the Pacific, thus gaining access to the riches of the Far East, that is, China. Because of Virginia's latitude, many thought that Virginia held the shortest route. Not much is known about John Lederer except that he was German, a physician, and baptized in the Evangelical-Lutheran church, Nicholas. He was the son of Johann Lederer and was born around 1644. Tax records from 1646 reveal that they lived in Hamburg. They also reveal that in 1657 authorities determined that his father was not paying enough taxes in regard to his income.[5]

On August 20, 1670, Lederer started his journey from below the falls of the Rappahannock River. His expedition consisted of nine colonists and five Indians. They were well organized and provisioned. The provisions not only included food, but plenty of alcohol for toasting. The colonists had horses to ride and the Indians walked.[6] The Indians were most likely guides and interpreters. Lederer did not know Indian sign language.[7]

---

4 Eugene M. Scheel, *Culpeper, A Virginia County's History Through 1920*, (Orange, Green Publishers, Inc., 1982), p. 4.
5 Douglas L. Rights and William P. Cumming, *The Discoveries of John Lederer*, (Charlottesville, Virginia University of Virginia Press, 1958), p. 71.
6 Ibid., p. 71
7 Ibid, p. 87-88.

One of the colonists, Colonel John Catlett, was a mathematician, a surveyor, and large landholder. He was a gentleman who lived downstream of the falls and owned several thousand acres on both sides of the river. Originally from Kent, England, he was made Justice of Rappahannock County. That part of Rappahannock County is now Caroline County. Catlett was also a Colonel of the local militia, which proved to be a precarious position. Soon after his return from Lederer's expedition he was killed by Indians while fighting with the militia.[8]

Lederer's group left from the house of Robert Taliaferro, a neighbor of Catlett. At that time there were no towns or cities in Virginia except Jamestown and Norfolk. Also, there were no real roads, just old Indian paths and farm lanes that connected the plantations to the Chesapeake Bay. The bay was the only viable transportation route. Naturally, Lederer would have followed the Indian trails on his journey. When the expedition arrived at the falls of the Rappahannock River, at present day Fredericksburg, they crossed and set up camp. The crossing was probably at the Indian fish traps of Mohaskahod.

The following day the expedition proceeded upstream, and according to Lederer's map, they used the same Indian trail that went to Hassininga, Amoroleck's village. It was the same trail that Amoroleck and other Hassininga Indians took to get to the fishing camp at Mohaskahod. Also according to the map, they recrossed the river about one mile upstream of the confluence of the Rappahannock and Rapidan Rivers, the location of Hassininga and Richards Ford. When they got to Hassininga the Indians were long gone, probably victims of disease, possibly introduced by Amoroleck's contact with John Smith.

There is a ridge, or spine between the Rappahannock and Rapidan Rivers that runs west from Richards Ford. At the crest of the spine is the present day village of Richardsville. After crossing the river, Lederer followed the spine, passing through the present day site of Richardsville, and searched for a place to camp. The site of Richardsville probably would not have been a suitable location. It had no water source.

Five days after leaving Richards Ford the party reached the crest of the first mountain range. They got off their horses and climbed the nearest peak. It is believed to be Compton Peak near Chester Gap, although there is a marker at Manassas Pass making the claim. Another claim has placed them at Harpers Ferry, although this is very unlikely. It all depends on which branch of the river they followed. Regardless, when they reached the top of the mountain range, they did not see a route to the Far East, only more and larger mountains. In turn, being cold and tired, and being late in the afternoon, they did what came natural. They drank a toast to the King.[9]

After returning, John Lederer settled in Maryland. In 1672, his observations were published by the governor of Maryland, Sir William Talbot.[10] Lederer went back to Germany in 1675.[11] Today, in the heart of Richardsville is a marker. It was placed there November 6, 1982 by the "National Society of Colonial Dames - 17th Century." The marker reads, *"John Lederer passed here August 21, 1670."*

---

8 Ibid., p. 87.
9 Ibid., pp. 89-90.
10 *The Early Discoveries of John Lederer*, 1644 <http://www.alexanderstreet2.com/EENALive/bios/A6812BIO.html>
11 Douglas L. Rights and William P. Cumming, *The Discoveries of John Lederer*, (Charlottesville, Virginia, University of Virginia Press, 1958), pp. 70-71.

Settlement

The land between the Rappahannock and Rapidan Rivers, near the confluence of the two rivers, was eventually obtained by a man named Simon Miller. He received it from a Lord Fairfax land grant. The King of England granted Lord Fairfax most of Northern Virginia. Fairfax later granted or sold tracts, with Miller obtaining one of them. In 1773, Simon Miller gave the land between the two rivers to William Richards when William married his daughter, Eliza. William was born in 1755 and was the son of John Richards. John was from Falmouth and owned a mercantile business in Fredericksburg.[12]

William built a house on the Culpeper side of the Rappahannock River, overlooking the ford. The place has since been called Richards Ford. The house was described by a Civil War soldier as a *"fine old Virginia Mansion."*[13] In reality it was a modest Virginia house. It had clapboard siding and stone chimneys on each end. The foundation was also stone. The front porch faced the river, and the entrance went into a hallway with rooms on each side. The staircase to the upstairs bedrooms was located in the hallway.

William was a wealthy man and owned land in many places. Some were large tracts, 100 - 300 acres, located in the counties of Spotsylvania, Stafford, Orange, Hampshire, and Culpeper. William even owned two tracts in Kentucky, one of which was 500 acres, and the other 50,000 acres. When he died in 1817, his will instructed that the land be sold to pay debts, and what was left go to his son James. His other son, William, had died in 1811, after going to Kentucky. William's will also instructed that the slaves were to be divided up among his children.[14]

James already had 800 acres at the ford conveyed to him by William before he died. James did not stay at Richards Ford, and ended up moving to Tennessee. After he died in 1837, his land at the ford was then divided up among his children.

The river mansion and 353 acres were inherited by his daughters Mollie M. and Eliza. Molllie M. was born in 1822 and Eliza was born in 1821. James had two other daughters, Harriet and Sarah. Harriet received 262 acres and Sarah received 141 acres. James's son, Benjamin Franklin, who was born in 1806, received forty-three acres and a house further inland, overlooking the Rapidan River.[15] It was about a mile from Richards Ford and may have originally been Simon Miller's house. Benjamin had twelve children, unfortunately nine of them died of typhoid fever.[16]

James's other son, William Thomas Jefferson (William T. J.), received 157 acres. He was born in 1801, and in 1827 married Ann Humphreys. He was the postmaster of Richardsville from June 14, 1831 to January 1, 1835. Sometime after 1842, William T. J. moved to Texas, where he died in 1886.

The original name of Richardsville was Smith's Tavern. The Smiths lived and operated a tavern there in the early 1800s. The first post office was established at Smith's

---
12 Interview with Fred Ricker, William Richards' descendent and Richardsville resident.
13 City of Fredericksburg, Virginia, *Historic Resources along the Rappahannock and Rapidan Rivers*, (Fredericksburg, Va., Billingley Printing and Engraving, 2002), p. 74.
14 Culpeper Connections, Journal of the Culpeper Genealogical Society, *Will of William Richards,* November 2003, Vol. 3, No. 2, pp. 44-47.
15 Culpeper County Deed Book 13, p. 509.
16 Interview with Fred Ricker, William Richards' descendent and Richardsville resident.

Tavern on December 15, 1828. The name was changed to Richardsville's Post Office March 8, 1831, after William T. J. became the postmaster.[17] Curiously, it is a wonder why the village was ever called Richardsville. The nearest Richard's house was more than five miles away. A more appropriate name would have been Smithville, or maybe Humphreysville.

Captain Thomas Humphreys owned the nearby plantation, "Locust Hill," on the Rapidan River. He married one of William Richards's daughters, Elizabeth, and they had fourteen children. In 1843, his son, John Humphreys, built a house at the village, and it survives as the oldest standing house in Richardsville. John was also one of the original members of Richardsville's Oakland Baptist Church. His grave marker is in back of the church, and is the only one that can still be identified. The initials JBH, A 72, 1884 are scratched on a fieldstone marking his grave. His wife is presumed to be buried next to him.

Road and Ford

On the south side of the river were two approaches to Richards Ford. They are both discernable because they form deep cuts in the bluff as they go down to the river. One came from the direction of Richardsville and passed by the original Richards house. The other came from the direction of Elys Ford, to the south.

Mills

In 1817, Richards Ford was surveyed for the upcoming Rappahannock River Canal Company. The survey showed that the Richards had a house, a mill, and a ferry. A later map made in 1845 by the Rappahannock River Canal Company locates two mills there.[18] They were a grist mill and a sawmill belonging to James Richards.[19] The mill lot consisted of a little over eight acres. When the mills ceased operation is not known.

Ferry

The ferry that operated at Richards Ford was first referenced in 1779 when the Virginia Assembly approved a discount rate of one shilling per man or horse to be ferried there. It ran from the land of Edward West, on the Stafford County side, to the land of Simon Miller, on the Culpeper County side. In 1792, the ferry was described as being between William Richards's land in Stafford County and Simon Miller's in Culpeper County. By 1818, the crossing was known as Richard's Ferry.[20]

Canal System

The Rappahannock River canal system arrived in the 1830s, and eleven acres of the Richards' land was condemned for a canal, locks and dam.[21] Canal records label this section as

17 National Archives and Records Service, *List of Postmasters*, Richardsville Virginia, Washington DC.
18 *John Couty, Rappahannock River Canal Improvements, 1845*, (Museum of Culpeper History, Culpeper, Va.).
19 Culpeper County Deed Book 9, p. 407.
20 Eugene M. Scheel, *Culpeper, A Virginia County's History Through 1920*, (Orange, Green Publishers, Inc., 1982), p. 135.
21 Culpeper County, Deed Book 13, p. 509.

Richards Dam and Powells Canal. Paine's 1862 map labels it Powells Dam. The dam was 200 feet long and 3.5 feet high. Three locks lowered the boats back into the river from the mile long canal that was 8 feet wide and 6 feet deep. The guard lock to the canal is still next to the river. The lowest lock was wooden and is silted over. The other two locks are in good condition.[22]

The canal was probably named after an adjacent land owner named Powell. Local tax records from 1850 lists an Elisha Powell owning 280 acres. The canal's stone work is impressive. There were actually two canals at the lower end. One was for the canal boats and the other was for the two mills that the Richards operated there. The inner canal was the one used for the navigation system.[23] Retaining walls were built to protect the canal from floods.

The river was backed up from a dam at the confluence, approximately one mile downstream. Hence the ford was flooded, allowing the Richards to operate a ferry there. With two major transportation routes going through, that is, the canal and the ferry, Richards Ford would have been a very busy place.

In 1847, an interesting situation occurred as a result of the construction and repairs to the canal. In the process of being upgraded and repaired, the Richards lost the water powering their mills. The road to the mills was also flooded. The Richards went to the Circuit Court and obtained an injunction to stop the work. An agreement was made in which the canal company could resume work, put up temporary shanties for the workers, and condemn close to thirteen acres of land for the canal system. In return, the company agreed to maintain a road to the mills, maintain a water source to the mills, and allow the Richards to build a bridge over the canal. The Richards also received $465.00.[24]

Civil War

By the time of the Civil War, the Rapidan River crossings at Elys and Germanna had diminished Richards Ford use. The Rappahannock River canal system was no longer operating and the dam a mile downstream was in disrepair. Because of this, the water levels were not always deep enough for the ferry to float, which made it undependable. Instead of a transportation route between Fredericksburg and Culpeper, the crossing was only used by local residents. This continued until 1862, then Richards Ford became a strategic military point for the next two years.

1862

In the summer of 1862, the Union army under General McClellan failed in its attempt to capture Richmond by the sea, and a new army was formed under General Pope. Pope's army was comprised of various smaller armies that had tried to defeat Stonewall Jackson in the Shenandoah Valley the previous June. Pope's plan was to drive on Richmond, using the Orange and Alexandria Railroad for his supply line. The route brought him over the Rappahannock River, and thus, the various river crossings became very important.

22 John Couty, *Rappahannock River Canal Improvements*, 1845, (Museum of Culpeper History, Culpeper, Va.).
23 City of Fredericksburg, Virginia, *Historic Resources along the Rappahannock and Rapidan Rivers*. (Fredericksburg, Va., Billingley Printing and Engraving, 2002), p. 74.
24 Culpeper County Deed Book 9, p. 407.

On July 12, 1862, Pope's army crossed the Rappahannock River and entered Culpeper County. During this campaign, Pope wanted the fords on the lower Rappahannock and Rapidan Rivers guarded. On July 25, 1862, Major General Irvin McDowell, whose forces were just transferred to Popes command, sent a report, "*. . . The full regiment of cavalry you sent from Washington to me day before yesterday has not been heard from. To use it to the best advantage for the purpose you have in view it should go to the United States or Richard's Ford on the Rappahannock.*"[25]

Earlier that day, Brigadier General Rufus King had also received orders from Pope to guard the lower fords on the rivers. He notified Pope that, "*Your dispatch received. We will continue to keep close watch of the fords near the fork of the Rapidan and Rappahannock, as well as the roads to our front. Our cavalry patrols go out every day. If any such movement as you suggest is attempted we can hardly fail to get timely notice of it.*"[26]

By early August, Pope's most advanced wing, under General Banks, was in Culpeper. On August 8, Banks left Culpeper and headed toward Orange. The next day he was stopped by Stonewall Jackson at the Battle of Cedar Mountain. Being driven from the field by Jackson's superior numbers, Banks retreated to Culpeper where they could be reinforced.

Nine days later, on August 18, Pope issued orders for the entire army to withdraw to the north side of the Rappahannock River. Robert E. Lee was advancing with a large Confederate army and Pope did not want to be caught between the Rapidan and Rappahannock Rivers. He had also just found out that Lee's plans included flanking him on his left. One of Jeb Stuart's staff officers, Captain Fitzhugh, was captured, and he had the orders outlining the plan in his dispatch case. Stuart narrowly escaped when Fitzhugh was captured, although he did lose his famed plumed hat.[27]

Pope's army crossed the river in three columns, one at Ellis (Barnetts) and Kellys Ford, one at Rappahannock Station, and the third at Sulphur Springs.[28] He then fortified the northern bank to await Lee. On August 22, General in Chief H. W. Halleck notified Pope that Porter's Corps had just arrived from McClellan's army, and they were being sent to reinforce him at Richards Ford. As of then, the only forces at Richards Ford were a small party of cavalry. Richards Ford itself was reported as "*. . . difficult, and the road connecting with the main road is blocked for a few miles.*"[29]

Halleck cautioned him, "*It is quite possible that the enemy, while making a demonstration lower down, may attempt to turn your position by Culpeper of Warrenton. If so, you will mass your force on the right and give him battle.*"[30] Halleck's concern about Pope's right flank was proven correct, however, the Confederates did not try to turn it; they went around it. By August 27, the Confederates were in Pope's rear, burning his supply trains at Manassas.

The Battle of Second Manassas followed, and then Antietam. After Manassas, Pope was replaced by McClellan, and on November 7, McClellan was replaced by General Burnside. Burnside, although reluctant to become the Union army's new commander, began to transfer troops to Fredericksburg for a drive on Richmond. By November 20, <u>Burnside's army</u> was poised across the river from Fredericksburg, waiting for pontoon

25 O.R., vol. 12, pt. 3, p. 506.
26 Ibid., p. 506.
27 Editors, *Lee Takes Command*, (Alexandria, Virginia, Time-Life Books, 1984), p.125.
28 O.R., vol. 12, pt. 3, p. 598.
29 Ibid., p. 621.
30 Ibid., p. 591.

boats. During the transfer of the troops, an interesting situation occurred involving Richards Ford and Burnside's nemesis, Joseph Hooker.

On November 19, General Hooker, who was in command of one of Burnsides three army wings, was protecting the army's rear. When he arrived at Hartwood Church, about six miles west of Fredericksburg, on the north side of the Rappahannock River, he sent a communication, *"I have the honor to request that you will call the prosecution of the campaign to allow my command to cross the Rappahannock River at the ford 4 miles distance from this point, and to march, by the most direct route, to Saxton Junction. I have three days rations from tomorrow morning, and forage I can obtain from the county. At Bowling Green I am nearer to supplies delivered at Port Royal than I can be here . . . "*[31] The ford that was four miles away was United States Mine Ford.

Not only did Hooker send this communication to Burnside, he went over Burnside's head, and sent a communication to the Secretary of War.[32] Regardless, Burnside did not approve the movement. He responded, *"From your position to Saxton Station, by way of United States Ford, is a distance of 36 miles, by way of Richards Ford and Ely's Ford on the Rapidan, is a distance of 43 miles . . . The United States Ford is said not to be passable for artillery of wagons. Richard Ford is represented to be poor, barely passable for artillery or wagons."*[33] Burnside was worried about Hooker getting too far away from his supply and the condition of the fords.

In retrospect, it might have worked. There was only cavalry at Fredericksburg, and Lee was more than thirty miles away at Culpeper. On the defense of Burnside, the rest of the army was across the river from Fredericksburg, waiting on pontoon boats. For all Burnside knew, Hooker could be trapped on the other side of the river by Lee's entire force. At any rate, even if the whole Union army was across the river, Lee would have more than adequate opportunities to block any drive to Richmond. This was demonstrated two years later during Grant's campaign.

On December 13, Burnside did cross the river at Fredericksburg and attack Lee. He failed to drive him from the field, and his army suffered terrible losses. After the battle, Burnside continued to hold the fords along the river and send out scouting parties. Colonel Di Cesnola, who was in charge of the cavalry, was ordered to keep Richards Ford and the road to Morrisville picketed.[34] Burnside then developed plans for a movement to get in Lee's rear.

It was to start with a cavalry raid. Crossing upstream on the Rappahannock at Kellys Ford, the troopers were to continue to Racoon Ford on the Rapidan River and then return. If nothing else, it was a probing action, although, the cavalry did take a contingent of, *". . . 20 well armed men, provided with means of destroying bridges, culverts, telegraph wires, etc."*[35] The raid was the prelude to Burnside's plan to march up the north side of the river and cross it to get behind Lee.

The commander of the cavalry that was assigned to this task was Brigadier General William Averell. On December 28, 1862, he sent a request that infantry accompany his troopers to Kellys Ford, but no further. As a diversion, Averell requested that a brigade of infantry cross at Richards Ford, march to Ellis Ford, and then recross the river.

31 O.R., vol. 21, p. 355.
32 Ibid., pp. 337-774.
33 Ibid., p. 104.
34 O.R., vol. 51, pt. 1, p. 958.
35 O.R., vol. 21, p. 896.

Burnside immediately sent orders to General Hooker to support Averell with an entire division. On December 29, 1862, he wrote, *"The commanding general directs that, instead of the brigade that was to cross the Rappahannock at Richards Ford, you detail a division... if found practicable, a brigade of this division should cross at Richards Ford, and return by Ellis ford."*[36]

The next day three brigades under Colonel James Barnes, who was in command of the 1st Division of the 5th Corps, left for Richards Ford. He sent one brigade, along with an artillery unit, to Morrisville. With the other two brigades, a detachment of 100 troopers from the 3rd Pennsylvania Cavalry, and 150 men from Berdan's 1st U. S. Sharpshooters, Barnes headed to Richards Ford. Fifty troopers, three companies of sharpshooters, and a brigade of infantry forced a crossing at the ford. Posted on the south side of the river were eight to ten pickets from the 1st South Carolina Cavalry. The South Carolinians were using the Richards' house near the ford as cover. The Berdan sharpshooters drove them away, but unfortunately, a female resident of the house was wounded. A soldier from the 118th Pennsylvania Volunteers wrote, *"Just on the edge of the ford stood a fine old Virginia mansion, occupied by a farmer and his three daughters. From the windows, the enemy had replied to the (Union) sharpshooters. In passing one of the windows, in search of a place of safety, one of the daughters was severely wounded in the thigh."*[37] Family history states that the girl was named Martha and she was wounded in the hip.[38] It is unknown who the farmer was, but Eliza and Molly M. Richards lived in the house at the time. A Civil War map labels the house as *"Miss Richards."*[39]

The other brigade then crossed and they all proceeded to Ellis Ford. The distance was about seven miles, although at that time it was believed to be around four. Before leaving, Barnes sent his medical director to attend to the wounded female at the house. As the column advanced, the South Carolina troopers would stop, fire, and retire. Barnes placed ten men of the cavalry in front to push them out of the way. He kept the Berdan sharpshooters on the column's flanks to act as skirmishers. Barnes's infantry brigade was never engaged.[40]

The South Carolina troopers that were guarding Richards Ford were also guarding Ellis Ford. In coordination with the Union column advancing from Richards Ford, a squadron of Union cavalry attacked from the northern bank of Ellis Ford. The southern troopers were pushed back as Barnes's soldiers came upon them from the rear. To avoid being caught between a cross fire, the South Carolinians fled. Unopposed, Barnes's soldiers crossed back to the north side of the river and joined the squadron of cavalry sent there to occupy the southern pickets. There are no reported casualties from this diversionary movement except for the female in the Richards' house. However, there were two southern pickets captured, along with their horses. One of the horses was wounded.[41] As stated before, these Union troop movements were diversions to Burnside's ambition of flanking Lee by crossing the river upstream of Fredericksburg.

---

36 Ibid., p. 897.
37 City of Fredericksburg, *Virginia, Historic Resources Along the Rappahannock and Rapidan Rivers.* (Fredericksburg, Va., Billingley Printing and Engraving, 2002), p. 74.
38 Interview with Fred Ricker, William Richards' descendant and Richardsville resident.
39 Schedler, J. engr., *Map of Culpeper County with parts of Madison*, Rappahannock, and Fauquier counties, Virginia. (Library of Congress).
40 O.R., vol., 21, p. 897.
41 O.R.., vol. 21, pp. 742-744.

The cavalry would sever the railroads supplying Lee's army while the infantry attacked Lee's rear. Burnside had gone as far as dispatching Hooker's division to support Barnes's reconnaissance when he was abruptly halted by President Lincoln himself. Lincoln sent a telegram instructing Burnside not to make any attack without his approval. The next day Burnside personally went by train to Washington. He obtained Lincoln's approval, but the delay and change of weather resulted in the famous "Mud March." Unrestrained, Burnside's earlier movement would not have been bogged down by mud, and might have worked. In May, after criticizing Burnside for the march, and now in command of the Union army, General Hooker implemented the same movement.[42]

1863

During the winter of 1863 the Union cavalry patrolled fords along the north side of the Rappahannock, from Kellys Ford to below Fredericksburg. The patrols sent to Richards Ford consisted of five to twenty-five men and were based out of Allcock, near Hartwood Church. They were part of a brigade of around 1,000 troopers, under the command of Colonel Di Cesnola, and made up the extreme right wing of the Union army. The brigade drew their supplies from the Falmouth depot.

In May, Hooker implemented Burnside's plan of marching up the north side of the Rappahannock River to cross and get behind Lee's forces at Fredericksburg. Two squadrons of cavalry were sent to Richards Ford to screen the army. Their orders were, *"to go to Richards Ford, and then work to the left until they found the infantry, and then to come as far north as possible."* [43]

After the Union army crossed at Kellys Ford, the 5th Corps was ordered to march to Chancellorsville by way of Richardsville. When they arrived at Richardsville, General George Meade, commander of the 5th Corps, made arrangements to secure his left flank. He sent detachments of the 8th Pennsylvania Cavalry to Ellis and Richards Fords. At Richards Ford the squadron surprised the Confederate picket and captured twenty nine soldiers.[44]

After the Union defeat at the Battle of Chancellorsville, the Union army recrossed the river at U. S. Mine Ford. Hooker instructed that his right flank be guarded at all costs. He ordered Major General Reynolds of the 1st Corps to send, *"the most reliable regiment (good shots), with a battery, to Richards ford, axmen with them, to fell trees, and make every possible obstacle to the passage of troops on our flank; to move quickly. The regiment and battery must intrench themselves, and be instructed   (confidentially) to fight to the death in case the enemy approach there."*[45] Hooker also ordered General Sedgwick to send some troops to Richards Ford. On May 5, Sedgwick sent Lieutenant Colonel Benjamin F. Harris and his 6th Maine Volunteers, where they remained until May 7.[46]

To further protect his right flank, Hooker ordered Brigadier Alfred Pleasonton to send a brigade of cavalry with a horse battery to obstruct all fords and possible

---
42 William K. Goolrick, ed. Time Life Books, *The Civil War, Rebels Resurgent,* (Alexandria, Virginia, Time-Life Books, 1985), p. 93.
43 O.R., vol. 25, pt. 2, pp. 275-276.
44 O.R., vol. 25, pt. 1, p. 506, p. 1079.
45 O.R., vol. 25, pt. 2, p. 420.
46 O.R., vol. 51, pt. 1, p. 187.

crossings from Richards Ford to Rappahannock Station. They were also instructed to take intrenching tools. Hooker's orders stated, "*Officers and men must be instructed to fight to the death to guard our right. Put most reliable and true men on this duty.*" [47]

Pleasonton sent a brigade under Colonel Davis and Martin's battery for the task. An additional horse battery was sent to cover Richards Ford. Hooker's fear that Lee would cross the river and attack his right flank never transpired. Lee's army was fought out.

The concern about the right flank continued. On May 28, Barnes's 1st Division of the 5th Corps was ordered to guard all the Rappahannock River crossings up to Kellys Ford. Barnes was also ordered to post at least a regiment with artillery at Richards Ford.[48] A few days later, on June 4, the entire 2nd Division of the 5th Corps, under Major General Sykes, was ordered to guard the Rappahannock crossings at Banks Ford and U. S. Mine Ford, and send detachments from a brigade posted at U S. Mine Ford to cover Richards Ford.[49]

One soldier with the 146th New York Infantry describes the duty, "*our life at Richards Ford was extremely wearing. While we were in camp we were kept busy building redoubts, rifle pits, and abatis, and were ready, at five minutes notice, to repel any attack on the ford or march to any point on the river. Each man was compelled to be out on picket duty every other day because of the great distance our regiment was patrolling. The pickets would lie in the back woods the greater part of the day, coming down to the river front at night. It rained frequently, rendering picket work doubly discomforting . . .*"[50]

The picketing continued until the armies departed on the Gettysburg Campaign. Not until late July did the troops return to the Rappahannock River. After Gettysburg, Lee retired back to the south side of the Rappahannock and concentrated his forces around Culpeper. The Union army, now under General Meade, followed. By July 18, Meade's army was on the north side of the river, with pickets from Richards Ford to U. S. Mine Ford.[51]

A few weeks later, on August 9, Lee withdrew to the south bank of the Rapidan River. His army could be better supplied there. Meade remained on the north bank of the Rappahannock until September 13. His cavalry then crossed and advanced into the town of Culpeper, where they drove the remaining Confederate cavalry out. During the street fighting the Confederates lost some artillery pieces, and Union Brigadier General Custer was shot in the leg, the only time he was wounded in the war.

Lee reported that on September 14, two Union army corps had crossed the Rappahannock, and the Union cavalry had been withdrawn from the lower Rappahannock. He also reported, "*some reduced pickets from Richards Ford to Fredericksburg.*" [52] Some of these pickets, a lieutenant and thirteen troopers belonging to the 1st Vermont Cavalry, were captured at Richards Ford on September 26. One of the troopers was killed and two escaped. They were surprised at four o'clock in the morning by Confederates coming

---

47 O.R., vol. 25, pt. 2, pp. 421- 422.
48 Ibid., p. 535.
49 O.R., vol. 51, pt. 1, p. 104.
50 City of Fredericksburg, *Virginia, Historic Resources Along the Rappahannock and Rapidan Rivers.* (Fredericksburg, Va., Billingley Printing and Engraving, 2002), p. 119.
51 O.R., vol. 29, pt. 2, p. 62.
52 Ibid., p. 720.

from Stafford Court House, which was in their rear. The Confederates boldly crossed the river with their prisoners in front of the pickets from the 8th New York Cavalry. According to the 1st Vermont's officer's report, "... *they were dismounted. They probably crossed the Rapidan near its mouth.* " [53]

Richards Ford was abandoned by the Union forces in mid October when Lee advanced on Washington during the Bristoe Campaign. It was, although, used briefly by escaping Union troopers under Captain Downing. They got separated from the rest of their force during the Confederate advancement through Brandy Station on October 11. The detachment had to ride all the way to Richards Ford to find a place to safely cross the river and reunite with the retreating Union army.[54]

In late October, a couple of Confederate guerrillas crossed at Richards Ford during a raid. One was from the 9th Virginia Cavalry and the other from the 1st South Carolina Cavalry. They captured six Union soldiers guarding some cattle at Weaverville, which was north of the river. With their prisoners, and captured horses, the Confederate raiders returned by way of the ford. One of the Union soldiers was able to escape.[55]

During the Mine Run Campaign, Richards Ford became important again. In November, Meade decided to cross the Rapidan River and attack Lee by a flanking maneuver to the east. Mine Run feeds into the Rapidan upstream of Germanna Ford. The Union troop movements brought their army across the Rapidan River at Germanna Ford and Culpeper Mine Ford. Two corps marched through Richardsville on the way to Culpeper Mine Ford. To screen the crossing, Union cavalry was sent to Richards Ford and beyond.

The Mine Run Campaign ended in failure for the Union army. Due to tardy troop movements by at least one of Meade's Corps generals, Major General French, Lee had the opportunity to have enough forces dug in across Mine Run to prevent crossing. An attack would have been futile and costly. The Union army returned to its camps around Brandy Station, and by December 3, settled in for the winter.

There was concern that the Confederates would attack the retreating army, so cavalry was stationed in the rear. On December 4, one full brigade of General Greggs 2nd Cavalry Division was posted at Richardsville, picketing the nearby fords. Also on December 4, a detachment of cavalry crossed at Richards Ford and proceeded to Hartwood Church. It was believed that if Confederate cavalry was to attack, it would be on the north side of the river. Nothing transpired, even though bushwackers were operating in the area.[56]

1864

The Union Cavalry Corps, consisting of three divisions, was assigned the task of picketing while the army was in its winter camps around Brandy Station, Rappahannock Station, and Culpeper. Greggs 2nd Cavalry Division was moved across the river to Morrisville, and the 3rd Cavalry Division, under General Kilpatrick, was assigned to picket the fords in the Richardsville vicinity. The specific cavalry picketing Richards

---

53 O. R., vol. 29, pt. 1, p. 198.
54 O.R., vol. 29, pt. 2, pp. 375-376.
55 Ibid., pp. 496-497.
56 Ibid., p. 541.

Ford consisted of the 2nd New York, 5th New York, and 18th Pennsylvania. Collectively they comprised the 1st Brigade under Brigadier General Henry Davies.

Throughout the winter, the 1st Brigade picketed the roads and fords around Richardsville. An 1864 military map shows that in March, forty-four men were stationed at Richardsville, a reserve of 100 men at Southard's Crossing (now the fire tower at Richardsville), nine men were posted at the intersection of Ellis Ford and Richards Ferry Road, and six men were assigned to Richards Ford itself. Mounted patrols, spaced thirty minutes apart, were sent on the connecting roads.[57]

The troopers stationed at Richardsville built winter huts in back of the Richardsville Methodist Church. Small rock piles are all that remain of the chimneys. Next to the church, buried in the field, is one of the soldiers that succumbed to illness during the winter.[58]

In April, Ulysses S. Grant was placed in charge of all the Union armies and he came directly to Culpeper to supervise Meade. Grant developed a plan to drive on Richmond and not turn back. To do so, Grant moved out of the winter camps, and marched on Lee's right flank. Grant's supply trains, more than 5,000, stayed east of the army to be protected. The route went to Richardsville, where they remained during the battle.

As a precaution for the drive south, orders were given to secure the fords round Richardsville. The 3rd New Jersey Cavalry was assigned Richards Ford.[59] With the fords secured, and the roads heavily patrolled, Grant proceeded with his plan. He drove south, crossed the Rapidan, and was attacked by Lee in the Wilderness. After the battle, the armies continued to maneuver south, fighting a series of battles. The further south they went, the less important Richards Ford became. After the Wilderness, no more records are found regarding its use during the Civil War.

Post Civil War

The Richards that remained after the Civil War consisted of Eliza, Mollie M., and Benjamin's family. Mollie Richards gave two slaves, Ned Hawkins and Mason Spilman, ten acre tracts of land each because they did not run away during the Civil War.[60] The Hawkin's house site is found past the gate at the end of Richards Ferry Road, about 200 yards on the left. It is on the City of Fredericksburg's land. The Spilman's tract is landlocked and closer to the original Richards' house.

The Richards were known as horse people and maintained a quarter mile horse track called "Horseshoe."[61] They also had a stud horse named "Alfred."[62] The agricultural records of 1880 show Eliza as owning twenty horses. 1850 tax records show Benjamin as owning one horse. In 1860 he had seven horses, but was down to three in 1870, most probably the result of the Civil War.[63]

---

57 *The Official Military Atlas of the Civil War*, (Washington, Government Printing Office,1895), plate LXXXVII.
58 Interview with Fred Ricker, William Richards' descendant and Richardsville resident.
59 O.R., vol. 36, pt. 1, p. 891.
60 Culpeper County Deed Book 19, p. 148, p. 29, p. 125.
61 Mary Stevens Jones, Richardsville, *Capital of Chinquapin Neck, Has Colorful History*, Culpeper Star Exponent, (Museum of Culpeper History, Culpeper, Va.).
62 Interview with Fred Ricker, William Richards' descendant and Richardsville resident.
63 Agricultural Tax Records, (Virginia State Library, Richmond, Va.).

Eliza died in 1900 and Mollie died in 1903. Benjamin Richards died in 1879.[64] They all are presumed to be buried in the family cemetery near the original Richards' house. Benjamin's sons, Samuel and John Royal, are buried there. Samuel's gravestone reads, "True Confederate Soldier." Obviously he served in the Confederate army, although company records of the local unit, Company E, 13th Virginia Infantry, do not list him. John Royal was the last of the Richards that lived in the area. He died of typhoid fever in 1906, at age 50.[65]

John Royal Richards's house stood on the left side of the road, about a half a mile before the ford. Later John Timberlake lived in the house. His parents, Ben and Melissa Timberlake, lived across the road. Rumors tell of John making whiskey. He married Ella Maupin, who lived upstream near Skinkers Ford. In the 1920s, Ella drowned while trying to cross the river at Richards Ford in a buggy. Ella Maupin Timberlake was buried in the family cemetery at the Maupin farm, next to her daughter that died at age eight. John Timberlake died in 1948, and then a man named David Mills lived in the house, but soon moved away.[66] The last person to live in the original Richards' house was Frederick Taylor, in the 1940s. The house was dismantled in the late 1980s, as it was unsafe. John Royal's house was intentionally burned down in the late 1980s because it was in such bad shape. The brick porch pillars of John Royal's house can be seen from the road. Deep in the woods is the foundation to Benjamin Richards's house, with the majestic view of the Rapidan River still evident. The area surrounding Richards Ford has reverted back to nature, mostly used for timber and hunting, with only the Richards' cemetery as evidence to the community once there.

In 1899, a novel called "Chickens Come Home to Roost," was written by L. B. Hilles. The novel uses Richards Ford as the backdrop, and some local people are said to be part of it. If you read carefully, a description of the house, canal, and roads can be found.

---

64 Culpeper County Birth and Death Records, vol. A-O, (Culpeper Library, Culpeper, Va.).
65 Interview with Fred Ricker, William Richards' descendant and Richardsville resident.
66 Ibid

Chapter Two

Emburys and Bells Ford

About a mile upstream of Richards Ford, just above Powells Canal, was Emburys Ford. It existed before the canal system was built. After the canal system, the ford would have been flooded, making it obsolete. It may have been usable again by the Civil War because most of the dams along the river were breached by neglect, floods, and ice. Emburys Ford was labeled as *"Emburys Old Ford"* by a Union Officer's report on the Rappahannock River crossings.[67] It is also identified on Captain W. H. Paines 1862 military map.[68] Approximately two miles upstream of Emburys Ford was Bells Ford. It was near the Crawley's Dam site, as labeled by Eugene Scheel's map of Culpeper County.[69] Not really a ford, the river could be crossed there at certain times of the year during low water. It was named after Richard Bell, who owned the property on the south (Culpeper) side of the river. Bell lived there during the 1800s and at least one Civil War map names the crossing after him.[70] It may have been used in the 1700s when a mill was located on the north side of the river. At any rate, it was only a local crossing, probably only used by the Bells because of the shorter distance to Goldvien as opposed to Richardsville.

Road and Fords

Emburys Ford crossed just upstream of Powells Dam, which was also called Richards Dam, below Lock 13. The route to Emburys Ford in Culpeper County is not confirmed. There is evidence of a road trace coming out of the bottom to the west of some steep cliffs. It could have connected to Route 619 or continued to Bells Ford Road. Paine's 1862 Civil War map shows two approaches to Emburys Ford in Stafford County. Powells Dam, built for the canal system in the 1830s, would have flooded the ford. That may be the reason it was called *"Emburys Old Ford"* in the Civil War.

The road to Bells Ford began across from the present day intersection of Richards Ferry Road (Route 619) and Beach Road (Route 743). After turning off Richards Ferry Road, and proceeding for about a mile, is the foundation of the Bell's residence. It is on the right side of the road, just before a creek. On the left side of the road is the Bells' cemetery.

Just past the Bell's house site, after crossing a creek, the road forks. The right fork possibly went to Emburys Ford. The left fork went to Bells Ford and connected to Mt. Ephraims Road. It was a way to the store, church, and post office at Goldvien.

---

67 City of Fredericksburg, *Virginia, Historic Resources Along the Rappahannock and Rapidan Rivers*. (Fredericksburg, Va. Billingley Printing and Engraving, 2002), p. 122.
68 Capt. W. H. Paine, A. D. C., *Map of part of Rappahannock River above Fredericksburg and the Rapid Ann River and the adjacent country*, Compiled under the direction of Col. J. N Macomb, A. D. C., Major Topi. Engrs., December 1862, Library of Congress.
69 Eugene Scheel, *Map of Culpeper County, drawn for the Second National Bank of Culpeper*, (Washington, D.C., William and Heintz, 1975).
70 J. Paul Hoffman, *Map of Orange County, Operations of Confederate and Union Forces*, by order Lt. Col. W. P. Smith, (Central Rappahannock Regional Library, Fredericksburg, Va.).

Mill and Canal

Crawley's dam and mill existed at the crossing in the 1700s. The mill was on the north side of the river. The dam was never part of the Rappahannock River canal system. This part of the river was flooded by the canal system's dam further downstream at Deep Run. The dam backed the river up to allow canal boats to float from Skinkers Ford to Deep Run.

Civil War

In 1858, Richard Bell purchased the land on the Culpeper side of the crossing from John Humphreys for $800.00 and built a house. At the time of the Civil War the Bell's farm encompassed around 280 acres.[71] The land across the river belonged to Edward Skinker.

Not until after the Battle of Fredericksburg, December 13, 1862, did the area become militarily important. To detect any troop movements upstream, Lee made sure all the crossings on the river were watched, including Bells. On January 13, 1863, Union cavalry pickets reported enemy pickets across the river at Bell's farm. Alfred Pleasonton, then a Brigadier General, reports, "*My pickets above report the enemy have placed pickets at Pie Island and Watson's Ford, about 2 1/2 miles above Richards Ford.*"[72] Pie Island is about a mile downstream of Deep Run. It is no longer an island, except in high water. Watson Ford may have been "Bells Ford."

Pleasonton also reports that Union pickets were deserting to the enemy above Pie Island. He writes, "*. . . one of General Averll's pickets left his post this morning between 4 and 5 o'clock; he connected to my right picket. The major thinks he has gone over to the enemy, and states that 2 men deserted from the same post two of three days ago.*"[73] The picket post could have been across Bells Ford or possibly further up at Skinkers Ford. In any case, it is curious. Possibly the slaughter at the Battle of Fredericksburg had something to do with it.

Being a tremendous vantage point to look across the river, troops spent the rest of the winter there. Lee, always cautious of an upstream crossing by the enemy, carefully guarded the fords along the entire river. Not only was it important for Lee to guard the crossings against the enemy surprising him, Lee used them to screen his actions. At the beginning of the Gettysburg campaign, Lee's invasion of the north involved marching his army west without the enemy discovering the movement. Bells Ford, with the commanding view from the Bell farm, would have been important in the screening operation.

Bells Ford only had minor importance during the rest of the war. Guerillas and scouts may have used it, and during the winter of 1863-64 Richard Bell may have worried about the Union troops stationed in the area. They were the same Union cavalry pickets that were stationed at Richardsville and picketing Richards Ford. Farms were often raided, and having two sons, George W. and William F., in the Confederate army, would have compounded his anxiety.

---

71 Culpeper County Deed Book 14, p. 4.
72 O.R. vol. 21, p. 968.
73 Ibid., p. 968.

His sons belonged to Company E, 13th Virginia Infantry, which was made up of local residents. George enlisted in Company E on April 3, 1862. He was captured on September 19, 1864 at Winchester Virginia and was sent to Point Lookout Prison until exchanged on March 15, 1865. William enlisted in Company E, or most likely conscripted, on March 18, 1863. He was wounded in the shoulder at Lynchburg on June 18, 1864 and later captured at Sayler's Creek on April 6, 1865. In 1904, William received the Cross of Honor at Fredericksburg.[74]

Post Civil War

Richard Bell continued to farm after the Civil War. Agricultural records in 1860 show that he had 141 improved acres and 141 unimproved acres, with a farm value of $915. He also had livestock valued at $304. Tax records of 1870 show that he had 100 improved and 176 unimproved acres, valued at $2108. Post war inflation had more than doubled the value of his land. The value of his livestock, however, was reduced to $240. The war had taken its toll. As of 1880, Bell had 85 improved and 185 unimproved, with a farm value of $2,160. Inflation had stabilized. Interestingly, each year the total acreage under cultivation was reduced.[75]

Richard Bell died in 1897, and his sons, William and George, sold the farm to Edwin Voegthy for $400. The farm consisted of 283 acres. Thirty four years later, during the Great Depression, Voegthy could not pay the taxes and the Culpeper County Treasurer seized the land. The property was bought at auction in 1952 with the payment of the taxes and penalties.[76] It is now in the Fred Kilsguard's estate.

Richards Bell's sons, William and George, moved to Fredericksburg and operated a furniture store.[77] George is reported living in or near Fredericksburg in 1908. The family graveyard is still across the road from the Bell house foundation. Heavily overgrown, it contains at least six graves. Some of the graves are obviously infants, revealing the mortality rates in 1800s. Richard and his wife are believed to be buried there.

---

74 David F Riggs, *13th Virginia Infantry*, (Lynchburg, Virginia, H. E. Howard, Inc., 1988), p. 101.
75 Agricultural Tax Records, (Virginia State Library, Richmond, Va.).
76 Culpeper County Deed Book 28, p. 115, Deed Book 131, p. 75, Deed Book 144, p. 302.
77 Interview with Fred Ricker, William Richards' descendent and Richardsville resident.

Chapter Three

Skinkers/ Rocky/ Martins Ford

Located five miles upstream of the confluence of the Rappahannock and Rapidan Rivers, and four miles upstream of Richards Ford, was Skinkers Ford. The ford was named after the Skinkers who owned land and mills on the north side of the river. Some Civil War maps label it as Rocky Ford.[78] Later, after the Civil War, the name changed to Martins Ford after Robert Martin bought a farm on the south side.

There was another minor crossing two tenths of a mile upstream, directly across the river from William Skinker's mill. The road to this unnamed crossing went through the farm of John Pemberton, which was known as "Oak Shade." Another lower approach to Skinkers Ford was at Thomas Pemberton's farm, "Peach Grove." The road trace still exists.

Skinkers Ford is well documented, first in a Rappahannock River Canal Company's map of 1845, and later in Civil War records. The general area includes the ford, the mills, the Rappahannock River canal system, and a local community.

Road and Ford

The road to Skinkers Ford is lined with large beautiful trees that canopy over. It passed by Robert Martin's house on the right and descended down a ravine, forming a deep cut. The erosion in the cut indicates much use. Once at the river, the ford went directly across too just upstream of Rock Run. Ultimately, the road went to Goldvein.

In 1845, the Rappahannock River Canal Company's engineer, John Couty, mapped the entire canal system. In the section of Skinkers Ford, he shows that the crossing was at the location of Martin's farm. His map also shows that on the north side of the river the road went over the canal and then crossed Rock Run by a bridge.[79] The bridge's location is still evident about a hundred yards upstream of where the run enters the river. Hotchkiss's map of Fauquier County also locates the ford directly across the river from the Martin farm. He labels it Rocky Ford. The map shows that the ford connected to the bridge across Rock Run and a road that went to Skinker's third mill.[80]

The road to the upper ford passed through a farm called "Oak Shade" before it crossed the river and went to William Skinker's mill. Oak Shade belonged to John Pemberton, Robert Martin's father-in-law. The approach to the river was not much more than a path, suitable only for pedestrians and horses. It went through a small ravine and was so lightly used that its trace can only be seen near the river. About a hundred feet downstream of the approach is a modern bulldozed road that also goes down to the river. A few hundred yards before the river crossing another road branches off to the left. A recent document has mislabeled this road as going to Skinkers Ford. The road did not go to the river, but crossed a creek and followed the ridge upstream. The road trace on the ridge is still evident.

---

78 Paul J. Hoffman, *Map of Orange County, Operations of Confederate and Union Forces*, by order of Lt. Col. W. P. Smith, (Central Rappahannock Regional Library, Fredericksburg, Va.).
79 John Couty, *Rappahannock River Canal Improvements,* 1845, (Museum of Culpeper History, Culpeper, Va.).
80 Jed Hotchkiss, *A Map of Fauquier County,* Virginia, Library of Congress.

The lower approach to Skinkers Ford that went through Peach Grove was also only suitable for pedestrians or horses. It either crossed to the mouth of Rock Run or followed the river upstream to Skinker/Martins Ford. If it crossed to the mouth of Rock Run, it would have been useable only during low water.

Mills

At various time periods, there were three Skinker's mills. All of them were on the north side of the ford. The first mill was built in the late 18th century. In August 1771, Fauquier County court records state, *"Thomas Skinker setting forth that he has Land on one side of Rock Run and intends to build a Water mill thereon and praying that an acre of Land may be laid off . . ."*[81] Thomas Skinker was a rich bachelor who lived in the Goldvein area. In 1790, he built a house near there and called it "Spring Hill." He died in 1803, but not before he built another house on Route 17 near Deep Run. It was named "Millburn."

The mill Thomas petitioned for in 1771 was built on the downstream side of Rock Run, just before it enters the river. On July 24, 1797, Thomas Skinker deeded the land between Rock Run and Deep Run to his nephew, William Skinker, Jr. William did not get the mill, though. The records state, *"excepting only out of the above my grist mill on Rock Run to my old and faithful servant Glosler during his life . . ."*[82] Slaves were often called servants.

William Skinker later built a second Skinker's Mill farther downstream, at the mouth of Deep Run. It was called Spring Mill. Court records show that William Skinker of Spring Hill and Thomas Brown of Mt. Ephraim made a request to build the mill on March 29, 1825. Then on February 27, 1827, Skinker made an application for a road to be built to their mill. Also in 1827, a reference is made to Skinker's, *"upper mill,"* indicating the first mill at Rock Run was still in use.[83] By 1828, Skinker and Brown had entered into a contract to operate the lower mill. An 1848 survey shows that Spring Mill was on Deep Run, just before it enters the Rappahannock River.[84] No records show that it was operated after the Civil War, which may have been its demise. The third Skinker's Mill, and the only one with walls still standing, was located about a quarter of a mile upstream of Rock Run. It was made out of stone, and the workmanship is impressive. The mill drew its water from the navigation canal that was built to allow canal boats to bypass the rapids. Evidently the third mill operated into the early 1900s, as deed records dated January 8, 1917 reference Skinker's Mill.[85]

On a bluff, a little upstream and overlooking the mill, stood a house. It may have been the mill's owner. Next to the house is a ravine where the road from the mill went to Pine View. Modern houses are now atop the bluff overlooking the mill. The mill and canal are on Fredericksburg property.

81 Ibid.
82 Lee Moffet, Water Powered Mills of Fauquier County, (Fauquier County Library, Warrenton, Va.), p. 134
83 *John Couty, Rappahannock River Canal Improvements, 1845*, (Museum of Culpeper History, Culpeper, Va.).
84 Lee Moffett, *Water Powered Mills of Fauquier County*, (Fauquier County Library, Warrenton, Va., 1974), p. 112.
85 Ibid., p. 134.

Canal System

The Rappahannock River canal system was extended to Skinkers Ford in the early 1830s. A dam was built at the head of a set of rapids, approximately a half mile upstream of the ford. It was 310 feet long, 8 feet high, and had two bends in it.[86] Stones from the dam can be seen on both banks of the river. The dam diverted water into a canal, which allowed canal boats to bypass the rapids.

Skinkers Canal was 3,800 feet long and located on the north side of the river. It began at the dam, just before a long narrow island is formed, and ended at Rock Run. The remains of the guard lock are at the entrance to the canal. About half way down the canal are the stone walls of William Skinker's mill. It drew water from the canal and discharged it back into the river. Further downstream, the canal went through a lock that lowered canal boats into Rock Run, by which they would enter the river. This lock is one of the best preserved locks of the river. It is completely intact and not silted in.

Ice and high water were a continuous problem in maintaining the operation of the canal system. The canal at Skinkers Ford was no exception. In 1834, the damage was so bad that it prevented boats from reaching Fredericksburg from Kelly's mill. The Virginia State Legislature came to the rescue and appropriated funds for repairs.[87]

Gold Mines

There were no gold mines in the immediate area of Skinkers Ford, although, the Union Gold Mine and the Johnson Gold Mine were inland, on Rock Run. The location of Union Mine is known, but the location of Johnson's Mine is not.[88] In Fauquier County, about two miles from the ford, is the village of Goldvein. It was originally called Grove Church, but was changed to Goldvein because of several mines near the village. The gold mining was so prevalent that Goldvein now hosts a gold mining museum.

Civil War

Lieutenant Lamuel B. Norton, signal officer in the Army of the Potomac, wrote that Skinkers Ford was, *"rocky, crossed by cavalry."*[89] One military map labels Skinkers Ford as a very bad ford.[90] Others label it as Rocky Ford. At any rate, if one wanted an example of a remote outpost during the Civil War, Skinkers Ford is it.

---

86 John Couty, *Rappahannock River Canal Improvements, 1845*, (Museum of Culpeper History, Culpeper, Va.).
87 Eugene Scheel, *Culpeper, A Virginia County's History Through 1920*, (Orange, Green Publishers, Inc., 1982), p. 147.
88 Eugene M. Scheel, *Map of Culpeper County, drawn for the Second National Bank of Culpeper*, (Washington D.C., William and Heintz, 1975).
89 City of Fredericksburg, Virginia, *Historic Resources along the Rappahannock and Rapidan Rivers*, (Fredericksburg VA., Billingley Printing and Engraving, 2002, P. 155.
90 A. H. Campbell, Captain Provisional Engineers and Lieutenant Dwight, Chief of Topl. Dept., C.S.P.E., *Survey of Culpeper and Madison Counties*, Va., 1863, Library of Congress.

1862

As remote and poor a crossing Skinkers Ford was, it was still used and guarded in the Civil War. General Pope would have secured it upon his retreat across the Rappahannock River after the Battle of Cedar Mountain. He crossed an entire division at Ellis Ford, two miles upstream. Once across the river, Pope's soldiers dug in.

Evidence of the defenses still exists. Until recently, on the Fauquier side of the river, above Skinker's third mill, was a short rifle trench. It is now obliterated by ATVs. Further downstream, just before Rock Run, downstream of the lock, is a cannon emplacement. The cannon emplacement points at both the river crossing of Martins Ford, and its approach from the bluff. Also, on the other side of Rock Run, near the bridge site, are the remains of a cavalry picket camp.

1863

After the Battle of Fredericksburg, Skinkers Ford was picketed by the Confederates. The picket camp was on the south side of the river at a vantage point that overlooked the ford. It also provided a commanding view upstream and downstream. They remained there until Lee moved out for the Gettysburg campaign.

After Gettysburg and Lee's retreat to Culpeper, the Union army followed, stopping at the Rappahannock River. The Union troops that took up positions on the north side of Skinkers Ford were the 149th New York Infantry, belonging to the 12th Corps. At the ford itself were cavalry pickets belonging to the 1st Vermont and 5th New York Cavalry. They were ordered to picket from Skinkers Ford to United States Mine Ford, and all the way to Potomac Creek.[91]

The 149th belonged specifically to the 3rd Brigade, 2nd Division, 12th Corps. The 3rd brigade was commanded by General George Greene. His headquarters was near Ellis Ford, about two miles upstream. On August 2, 1863, Greene reported, "*At Mr. Royal's one mile and a half below, is posted a detachment of 30 men, guarding a ford and dam.*"[92] This was Skinkers Ford. Royal had a house on the north side of the river near the third Skinker's Mill.[93] On the other side of the river were Confederate guerrillas.

On September 1, 1863, using Skinkers Dam, a group of Confederate guerrillas crossed in the night and killed one of the Union cavalry pickets. They scattered the rest of the pickets before returning back over the dam. The attack caused a stir and is documented in the Official War Records. A report from Jonathan Geary of the 12th Corps states:

"*I have the honor to state for the information of the General Commanding the Corps that Gen Greene reported to me at 7:30 O'clock last evening that the Cav pickets at Skinkers Dam about a mile below Ellis Ford were being fired upon. His brig was put under arms and Maj Thomas with 100 men of the 149th NY was sent to that point to recon discovering that the Rebs to the number of 10 to 15 crossed on the dam attacked*

---

91 O.R., vol. 27, pt. 3, p. 829.
92 Ibid., p. 829.
93 Captain V. E. Von Koerber, , *The Official Military Atlas of the Civil War, Map Showing the Picket Line of the First and Third Cavalry Divisions, Cavalry Corps, Army of the Potomac*, (Washington, Government Printing Office 1891-1895).

the pickets and after killing one scattering the rest they recrossed. Maj. Thomas has been ordered to remain there until relieved by an Inf force to be sent from U. S. Ford by Gen Warren. He has discovered no enemy and the lines have been quiet since his arrival. I have just returned from a visit to the lines and find from my officers statements there are about 300 Cav in our front between Ellis and Kemper Ford and by indication I judge there is also a section of artillery. These movements and changes of the enemy are evidently in apprehension of some movement on their part at the present."[94]

1864

After the Bristoe and Mine Run Campaigns, Lee's army settled in on the south side of the Rapidan River for the winter. The Union army went into winter camps along the Orange and Alexandra Railroad in Culpeper County. They maintained outposts along the Rappahannock and Rapidan Rivers throughout the winter.

Along with the other fords in the area, Skinkers Ford was heavily picketed until spring of 1864. The pickets were the same as those at Richard and Bells Ford, those belonging to Brigadier General Henry Davies 1st Cavalry Brigade. Ironically, some of the troopers, the 5th New York Cavalry, were the same troopers that picketed the other side of the river the previous August. Their familiarity with the fords may have been the reason for their assignment.

Confederates guerrilla activity continued. Locally, a guerrilla named Bill Thorn became famous, and a couple of stories involving him have been passed down by a nearby farmer, Edward Eley. His grandson Carl Eley tells:

"William (Bill) Thorn was a farmer that lived in the area, probably near the Rappahannock River, above Kellys Ford, on the Fauquier side. Being a loyal Virginian, he had a bitter dislike of Union soldiers, primarily because of their invasion of his home. Apparently he decided to carry on a one man private war with the enemy that occupied this land. Bill had many friends and admirers who agreed with his persistence and methods in causing as much trouble and pain as possible to the Yankees. One such friend was Edward Eley who had a farm on the north side of the Rapidan River approximately two to three miles above the forks of the two rivers. The road to the ford on the Rapidan (probably Blind Ford), ran through Mr. Eley's farm. Just by the front of his home, the gate and entrance to his farm being about a quarter mile and in plain view of his home.

On one occasion, Mr. Eley standing in his yard saw four men on horseback coming through the field gate. When they arrived at the house he saw that it was Bill Thorn with three Union soldiers, all of whom were roaring drunk. After a brief conversation, they continued on down the hill towards the river. Late in the afternoon, just before dark, Mr. Eley saw one man on horseback leading three horses coming back up the hill from the river. It was Bill minus the three soldiers. The three horses all had rifles and boots tied to the saddle, when Mr. Eley asked Bill about the soldiers, he replied "back down thar somewhere," pointing in the direction of the river.

On another occasion, Bill came riding into Mr. Eley's home, tired and almost give out, his horse foaming at the mouth. He had been riding hard. He told Mr. Eley the Yankees are after him and he needed a bite to eat and to rest a bit. After eating, he laid down in front of the fireplace and immediately fell asleep. In a few minutes Mr. Eley

---

94 O.R., vol. 29, pt. 2, pp.151-152.

looked out the window and saw a group of soldiers coming through the field gate. He very quietly awoke Bill and warned him. Bill quickly ran out the back door, down past the barn, and hid in the woods. Mr. Eley went out and greeted the soldiers. The officer in charge asked Mr. Eley if he had seen Bill Thorn. Mr. Eley replied he had not. The officer then told him, "when you see Bill Thorn you tell him I have sworn to get him and when I do, I intend to hang him to the nearest tree." Apparently he never did catch Bill since there is evidence that Bill survived the war, went back to his farm, and did well."[95]

Post Civil War

At or near Skinkers Ford, on the south side of the river, lived the Pembertons, Martins, and Maupins. One of the original settlers, Larken Pemberton, had a large farm nearby called "Orchard Farm." It was about two miles from Skinkers Ford and close to Edward Eley. The farm house was built around 1803 and had a fireplace so large a person could stand in it. Generations of Pemberton's lived in it but by the early 1900s the house stood vacant. Finally, in the 1930s it was dismantled.

In 1910, another house was built near Orchard Farm by Harold S. Marean. The builder was Burruss Walker, a well-known local carpenter. Burruss initially stayed in the Orchard Farm house while he constructed Marean's, but soon moved out. He proclaimed it was haunted.[96]

The family graveyard at Orchard Farm still exists. The only readable marker in the graveyard is Major William P. Newby, born 1785, died 1847. Newby was Larkin's son-in-law. The last person buried there was in the 1930s. He was a logger who lived in a nearby worker's shanty. He was often invited to dinner by Rosser Timberlake, who lived near Edward Eley's house. One time the logger did not show up, so the next morning Rosser went to check on him. He was found in bed, having intentionally swallowed some poison. The logger was still alive but soon died.[97]

Just upstream of Skinkers Ford lived Larkin's son, John Pemberton. The land he lived on originated as part of the Captain Thomas Humphrey's estate. Thomas obtained the tract of land from William Richards when he married his daughter, Elizabeth. Thomas died in 1848, and in 1857 the land was divided up into thirteen lots and allocated among the Humphrey's family, some being quickly sold. All the lots were thirty-nine acres, except for one, which was one hundred and eleven acres. The one hundred and eleven-acre tract was given to John Pemberton because he married Thomas Humphrey's daughter, Elizabeth. John named the farm "Oak Shade."

On the southeast corner of Oak Shade lived John's daughter, Sallie. She lived in a log house with a large stone fireplace. Later, a German lady by the name of Benedict lived with her. Sallie never married and died in the early 1900s. Local lore tells about Sallie complaining of Civil War soldiers digging up the potatoes in the garden and that the soldiers moved through in waves. The house stood until the 1930s, when it fell in on itself.[98] The large stone chimney still stands.

---

95 As told to Fred Ricker, William Richards' descendant and Richardsville resident, by Carl Eley, Edward Eley's grandson.
96 Interview with Fred Ricker, William Richards' descendant and Richardsville resident.
97 Ibid.
98 Ibid

There is a graveyard in front of Sallie's house. Besides members of the family, local legend tells of a Union soldier being buried there. He was found dead in a tree, possibly a sniper. There was some contention between the family members as what to do with him. Some members of the family did not want a "Yankee" buried in the family plot. Others felt they had to do something with him. At any rate, he is said to be buried in the graveyard.

Next to Sallie lived Robert Martin and her sister Eliza Pemberton. Robert married Eliza in 1869. In 1872, he bought a 39-acre lot adjoining Sallie's for $119. Robert built a house made of logs, and it still stands next to the road that goes to Martins Ford. The lot was given to Sallie by Colonel W. S. Kemper, who was married to Sallie's aunt, Sarah Humphreys. W. S. Kemper is not to be confused with the famous Confederate general and governor, James Lawson Kemper. W. S. Kemper's daughter, Charlotte Kemper, became a missionary in Brazil. Unfortunately she died there.

On the property next to Robert Martin's farm, on the downstream side, is a depression indicating where a building once stood. It is not known if it is a house site or a barn. From the depression is a worn path going down a ravine to the river, then it may have crossed to the mouth of Rock Run. This was the lower crossing below Skinkers Ford that went through Thomas Pemberton's farm, "Peach Grove."

Thomas was John Pemberton's son and the brother of Robert Martin's wife, Eliza. In 1860, Thomas Pemberton bought the hundred-acre farm and called it "Peach Grove."[99] He built a house that sat on the bluff overlooking the river. It was a typical farmhouse with a gable roof and kitchen that faced the river. He had five children and four slaves. Four of the children were girls.[100]

During the Civil War, Thomas Pemberton and his brother, Billy, served in Company E, 13th Virginia Infantry. They enlisted May 1862. Billy was made sergeant and was wounded twice, first at Gaines Mill and then at the Battle of Fredericksburg. He was recommended for promotion to 2nd Lieutenant after the Battle of Cedar Mountain. Billy was also cited for distinguished service at Fredericksburg during the Chancellorsville Campaign. At the Third Battle of Winchester he was mortally wounded. Later, Thomas was captured at High Bridge during Lee's retreat to Appomattox Court House. He was sent to Point Lookout Prison, where he remained until he took the Oath of Allegiance, June 16, 1865.[101]

After the war, Thomas was said to be cantankerous and very hard to get along with. At one point, Thomas encountered Robert Martin on a path downstream of Robert's house and a scuffle ensued. Thomas ended up cutting Robert Martin's riding boot with a knife. The boot was the type that folded down.[102] It may have been about livestock escaping and trespassing. On September 29, 1889, Robert served legal notice stating, *"I hereby give you lawful and legal notice - that 6 months from date - I refuse to join fences with you in the line fence from the river."*[103]

Thomas was married to Anne Bullard and evidently they did not get along. After she died, Thomas could be seen at her grave cursing her. Anne's grave is the only one

---

99 Culpeper County Deed Book 14, p. 374.
100 Interview with Fred Ricker, William Richards' descendant and Richardsville resident.
101 David F. Riggs, *13th Virginia Infantry*, (Lynchburg, Virginia, H. E. Howard, Inc., 1988), p. 134.
102 Interview with Fred Ricker, William Richards' descendant and Richardsville resident.
103 Legal notice of Robert Martin in author's possession.

located in back of the Richardsville Methodist Church. Thomas is buried in the Baptist cemetery across the road from Oakland Baptist Church.

In 1902, Thomas deeded 50 acres of Peach Grove, including the house, to his daughter Minnie and her husband, Horace Maupin.[104] Horace was old enough to have fought in the Civil War but there are no records of him being in the local unit, Company E, 13th Virginia Infantry. Minnie died in 1940, still complaining about the "Yankees" tearing open their mattress and also stealing their chickens and cows.[105]

The Maupin's daughter, Ella, married John Timberlake of Richards Ford. As previously mentioned in the Richards Ford chapter, Ella drowned during the 1920s, while crossing the river in a buggy at Richards Ford,. Ella is buried next to her parents in the Maupin graveyard near the Pemberton-Maupin house site. Her daughter, who died at age seven or eight, is also buried there. The house at Peach Grove survived until the late 1980s, when it was burned down because it was considered a nuisance.

Another daughter of Thomas's, Lucy Pemberton, lived on one of the 39-acre lots of the Humphrey's estate, just on the other side of Oak Shade. The lot was inherited by Flodoardo H. Humphreys, who built a house there. In 1890, he sold the house to Thomas. Just prior to the Civil War, Flodoardo moved across the river with his wife, Judith, built another house, and was the superintendent of the Franklin Gold Mine. Flodoardo eventually died of stomach cancer, just a few days after his wife died. As requested, he was buried in the same grave as his wife.[106] Thomas Pemberton passed the house on to his daughter Lucy. She lived in the house until the 1940s. It stood until the 1970s. In front of this house stands the Haydn house, which was once a sawmill operated by Murry "Buck" Martin. It can be seen from Route 683.

Present

Skinkers/Martins Ford provided a shorter distance to a store, a post office and a church at Goldvein, less than two miles away. Richardsville was almost four miles away. Skinker's third mill only lasted while the canal functioned. With the advent of motorized vehicles, the crossing became obsolete.

The only farm that remains is Robert Martin's. It was continually lived in throughout the years, and its structures, that is, the log house, a cottage, two barns, and an ice house, remain. Next to the ice house is a well lined with stones. The very top stone has the date September 13, 1894 scratched in it. The Martin farm has since become the Rappahannock River Campground.

In the river, in front of Martin's farm, is a large rock. Standing on the rock, looking upstream, the river descends through rapids dotted with small islands. Looking downstream from the rock is the ford. It is a serene place with a tall cliff towering above. In the evening, after working the farm, Robert would sometimes sit on the rock, sipping home brew, and reflect. And from time to time, at the end of the day, each consecutive owner of the property has done the same.

---

104 Culpeper County Deed Book 28, p. 273.
105 Interview with Fred Ricker, William Richards' descendant and Richardsville resident.
106 Koplend Geneology, <http//home.swbell.net/Koplend>

Chapter Four

Ellis Ford

Ellis Ford, located seven miles above the confluence of the Rappahannock and Rapidan rivers, has a recorded history that goes back to the early 18th century. Prior to that, local Manahoac Indians inhabited the area and used the rapids above the ford for fish traps. By the 1800s, Ellis Ford was one of the busiest crossings on the river. It had mills, a ferry, a village, a post office, a canal system, and several nearby gold mines. During the Civil War, Union and Confederate armies used and guarded it extensively. It was during this period that Ellis Ford was best documented. Eventually a bridge upstream at Kellys Ford made the crossing obsolete, and it faded into history. Now Ellis Ford has reverted back to a remote wilderness area, only accessible by the water, and displaying a natural beauty that makes it one of the most scenic places on the Rappahannock River.

Road and Ford

The ford was at the end of a slender island, just after a set of rapids. It is, without question, one of the most picturesque sites on the river. Looking upstream, the river comes cascading through a set of rapids. Looking downstream, the river is serene. The remoteness just adds to the beauty. Ellis Ford epitomizes how special a river can be.

On the south side of the river, the road from the ford traversed downstream for about a quarter of a mile, crossed a canal, and followed a creek inland. Large sections of the road had planks of timber laid across it to aid in traversing the ruts and potholes.[107] The bluff next to the road is impressive. It is very steep, very high, and very commanding. Old growth trees form a canopy, filtering the sun, making it somewhat surreal.

At the base of the bluff, just before the road turns inland, is a canal lock. Just after the lock the road crossed the canal. Dirt abutments from the bridge remain. After the canal was abandoned, it is evident that the road crossed through it, instead of over it. Once across the canal the road followed a creek for a few hundred yards, and then split. One road went straight up the bluff, resulting in a deep cut. The other road veered left, continuing past the Staunton-Barnett's house. On the north side of the river, the road went past Ellis's mill and house. It then went up a ravine, forming a deep cut. A stone foundation is adjacent to the road just before it goes up the ravine. It may have been a toll booth. The road ultimately went to Pine View.

Mills

The ford at the end of the rapids is where the river becomes shallow and sandy. The location made it a suitable to place mills because the fall of the river could power them. For two hundred years various mills were located there, with at least ten different owners.

---

107 Eugene M. Scheel, Culpeper, *A Virginia County's History Through 1920*, (Orange, Green Publishers, Inc., 1982), p. 143.

The first Staunton's Mill was on the south side of the river in Culpeper County. In front of the mill is a slender island.[108] The south channel around the island was damned up to divert water into the mill. It operated in the 1700's and was identified in a 1776 map drawn by Eugene Scheel. A 1737 Lord Fairfax survey map of northern Virginia locates the Staunton's house on a bluff just east of the mill site.[109]

Sometime before 1791, William Richards bought the mill, house, and surrounding land from William Staunton.[110] Richards later gave the mill to Benjamin Barnett after he married his daughter, Isabella.[111] From then on it was called Barnett's mill. The earliest record of Barnett's Mill is in 1809, when Barnett asked the court, *"for a road from Field's Ford to Barnett's Mill, formerly Stanton's Mill and from said mill to Grove Meeting House."*[112] In 1817, a map prepared by State Engineer Laozi Baldwin identified Barnett's Mill and house located at the same site as Staunton's.[113] Now, all that remains of the original Staunton - Barnett's mill are some scattered stones.

Some time after 1829 Barnett moved the operation to the other side of the river, probably because of a canal system being constructed on the south side.[114] There was already another mill across the river, built in the late 1700's. In 1791, Thomas Fallis was authorized to build a mill on his land at *"Rattle Snake Castle."* William Richards, who owned Staunton's Mill across the river, immediately took him to court. Richards claimed that Fallis's Mill would divert water from his mill. The courts ruled to allow Fallis to raise his dam, *". . . to a rock standing in the river, called blue rock, which joins Mr. Richard's summer dam . . ."*[115]

On January 17, 1833, Fauquier County deed records state that Benjamin N. Barnett sold a grist and sawmill to John. J. Royall, the highest bidder. It continued to be called Barnett's Mill though, because on October 27, 1835 Fauquier County court records refer to, *"road leading from Barnetts Mill."*[116] Benjamin Barnett, Sr. died in 1835, and Benjamin Barnett, Jr. was made his will's executor.[117] Benjamin Sr. would have been around 68 when he died because Culpeper's 1810 census lists his age as 44. The census also shows 4 males, 1 female, and 11 slaves in the household.[118]

---

108 Lee Moffett, *Water Powered Mills of Fauquier County*, Virginia, (Fauquier County Library, Warrenton, Va., 1974), p. 112.
109 *1737 Lord Fairfax Survey of Northern Neck, Virginia*, (Central Rappahannock Regional Library, Fredericksburg, Va.).
110 Lee Moffett, *Water Powered Mills of Fauquier County*, Virginia, (Fauquier County Library, Warrenton, Va., 1974), p. 114.
111 Culpeper Connections, Journal of the Culpeper Genealogical Society, *Will of William Richards*, November 2003, vol. 3, no. 2.
112 Lee Moffett, *Water Powered Mills of Fauquier County, Virginia*, (Fauquier County Library, Warrenton, Va., 1974), p.112.
113 Laozi Baldwin, State Engineer, *1817 map of Rappahannock River*, (Central Rappahannock Regional Library, Fredericksburg, Va.).
114 Fauquier Bicentennial Committee, *Fauquier County 1759 - 1959*, (Warrenton, Va., VA Publishing, 1959), p. 101.
115 Lee Moffett, *Water Powered Mills of Fauquier County, Virginia*, (Fauqueir County Library, Warrenton, Va., 1974), p. 114.
116 Ibid., p. 112.
117 Culpeper County Will Book.
118 Culpeper County 1810 Census.

Oddly, in November 1836, William K. Smith sold Benjamin Jr. land on the Rappahannock River including, "*a large manufacturing mill . . . millers house . . . to the mouth of a run called Adams Branch.*"[119] Evidently the mill was sold to Smith before Benjamin Jr. bought it back. He still owned it in 1837. In that year the Rappahannock River Canal Company reported that the canal system extends twenty miles to "*Barnett's Mill.*"[120]

Sometime before 1848, the mill and ten acres were purchased by Lewis Ellis.[121] The purchases were the result of a court case involving Hackley vs. Barnett.[122] At any rate, the Barnetts remained across the river in Culpeper County until at least 1860. The Richardsville tax records of that year list Barnett and sons as owning sixty acres of improved land. The 1870 tax records no longer list any Barnetts.

Lewis Ellis was the fifth owner of the mill on the north side of the river. The mill and community around it became known as "Mill Bank" and a ferry was also operated there.[123] By 1849, Mill Bank had a post office and H. A. Embrey was the postmaster.[124] Evidently the mill burnt down in 1855. The Fredericksburg Virginia Herald reported on April 9, 1855, that Lewis Ellis, owner of the mill, rebuilt it after a fire.[125] He may have borrowed money to rebuild the mill because in 1856 he was released from a debt that he took out on the mill and surrounding land.[126]

The mill was still operating at the time of the Civil War. A Union soldier stationed there in 1863 wrote:

"*The river at this point is not more than sixty feet wide, the highway leads down to it on either side, and the people riding on horse- back or in wagons ford the stream . . . Immediately at the ford there is considerable cleared land on both sides of the river, and rows of bushes and trees stand on the margins of the stream and in the gulfs where the brooks run down to the hillsides. The course of the river is somewhat tortuous, adding beauty to the scenery. An old man by name Ellis had his residence on the road . . . where it approaches the river. Just above, on the same side, were several buildings, shops, and a grist mill, belonging to the old man Ellis.*"[127]

An interesting account about one of Lewis Ellis's slaves is found in the book "Seasons of War." The book explains that one of Ellis's slaves attacked, or most probably fought back against Ellis's overseer, Heflin. As punishment, the slave was sentenced to be sold outside

---

119 Lee Moffett, *Water Powered Mills of Fauqueir County, Virginia*, (Fauquier County Library, Warrenton, Va., 1974), p. 112.
120 Fauquier Bicentennial Committee, *Fauquier County 1759 - 1959*, (Warrington, Va., VA Publishing, 1959), p. 110.
121 John Couty, *Rappahannock River Canal Improvements, 1845*, (Museum of Culpeper History, Culpeper, Va.).
122 Lee Moffett, *Water Powered Mills of Fauquier County, Virginia*, (Fauqueir County Library, Warrenton, Va., 1974), p. 113.
123 *Map of a part of the Rappahannock River above Fredericksburg and the Rapid Ann River and the adjacent country,* <http://cweb2.loc.gov/cig-bin/map-item.pl> December 1862.
124 Fauquier Bicentennial Committee, *Fauquier County 1759 - 1959*, (Warrington, Va., VA Publishing, 1959), p. 96.
125 City of Fredericksburg, Virginia, *Historic Resources along the Rappahannock and Rapidan Rivers*, (Fredericksburg ,Va., Billingley Printing and Engraving, 2002), p. 77.
126 Lee Moffett, Water Powered Mills of Fauquier County, Virginia, (Fauqueir County Library, Warrenton, Va., 1974), p. 113.
127 George K. Collins, *Memoirs of the 149th Regiment, New York Volunteer Infantry,* (Syracuse, 1891), p. 172.

the United States. This could have meant territories beyond the Mississippi River, or even worse, a sugar plantation in the Caribbean, which meant being worked to death.[128]

Lewis Ellis was very well off. Tax records of 1860 show that he owned 1100 acres in Culpeper County and another 200 in Fauquier County. The land in Culpeper County was worth $10,800, and the Fauquier land was worth another $9,000. All his livestock were on the Fauquier land, which included 20 horses, 68 cows, 12 oxen, 125 sheep, and 150 swine. The value of the livestock was another $5,000. The land in Culpeper County was evidently mostly wooded with 500 acres farmed. The records show that the 200 acres in Fauquier County produced ten times more than the Culpeper land.[129]

Lewis Ellis never married, and records do not show him as having any children, but he did have an illegitimate son. His mistress, Martha Martin, lived across the river near Skinkers Ford, and in 1847 they had a son named Robert Martin. She was sixteen years old and Lewis was fifty-one.[130] Robert lived first with his mother and later at Mill Bank. In 1866, he married Eliza Pemberton of Skinkers Ford. In 1872, they moved to land they bought from Eliza's sister, Sallie, next to Oak Shade at Skinkers Ford. It was also across from his mother, Martha. The farm is now known as the Rappahannock River Campground.

Lewis Ellis died August 3, 1869, at age 73.[131] As stipulated in his will, he is buried in the Fredericksburg Cemetery off of William Street. The will also releases Robert Martin of a debt to him, but ironically, the will lists Robert Martin as his nephew.[132]

On December 22, 1869, the mill was sold to Lewis and Isabella Brinkerhoff. An 1876 Fauquier County map labeled the mill as Brinkerhoff's. Lewis Brinkerhoff died in 1881, and after his wife remarried, the mill was sold to the highest bidder, Robert and Hezekiah Embrey. From then on it was called Embrey's Mill and continued operation until at least 1910. On March 27, 1911, the Embreys sold the mill to M. L. Johnson, who in the same day sold it to the Fredericksburg Power Company.[133]

There are various dates as when the mill ceased to operate, but they all agree that it burned down. One states it was 1913, another 1920, and another during a drought in 1931, when a forest fire moved through the area. A local resident describes Embrey's Mill as wooden, five stories high, and having four mill stones. It was the first mill in the area to make processed flour. There were several buildings used for wagons, barns, hen houses, a meat house, and a store operated by the Embreys.[134]

The remains of Ellis - Embrey's Mill are still present. The mill site has a 42 by 42 foot stone foundation with a large steel pipe in it. The walls vary in height from two to five feet. The mill race goes up the north side of the river, but disappears about half way to Snake Castle Rock, evidently washed away. Snake Castle Rock is a large rock outcropping and a dam site. Some stone work can be seen, along with a channel blasted through Snake Castle Rock. The channel diverted water into the mill race.

---

128 Daniel E. Sutherland, *Seasons of War*, (New York, NY, The Free Press. 1995), p. 15.
129 1860 Tax Records, (Virginia State Library, Richmond, Va.).
130 1870 Census Records of Culpeper County, (Bountiful, Utah, Precision Printing, 1989).
131 Lewis Ellis Headstone, (Fredericksburg, Virginia Cemetery).
132 Fauquier County Will Book, (Fauquier County Library, Warrenton, Va.).
133 Lee Moffett, *Water Powered Mills of Fauquier County, Virginia*, (Fauquier County Library, Warrenton, Va., 1974), p. 113.
134 Ibid., p. 113.

At least three more foundations are just above the mill site, one of which was Ellis's house. Further east of the mill, across a small stream, is a deep excavation near the base of the river bluff. It may have been for wagons to back into for a loading dock. There is the trace of another road that approaches from the downstream side of the river. It is probably a more modern access.

Canal System

The Rappahannock River Canal Company built a dam at Snake Castle Rock, almost a half mile upstream from Ellis Ford. It was 5 feet high and extended 412 feet diagonally across the river. On the south side of the dam was a guard lock made of wood and the beginning of a canal that allowed boats to bypass the rapids. At Barnett's mill, just before the boats returned to the river, the canal went through a rock outcropping that extended from the bluff to the river. Here the canal is irregular and bent, showing the difficulty of blasting a canal through it. On top of the bluff, just in back of the canal cut, is a flattened area which may have been Civil War defenses. A well-worn path goes up the bluff to this site.[135]

Near the end of the canal were two locks that lowered the boats back into the river, via a nearby stream. The first lock was made of wood with large cut stone ends. The gates have collapsed into the lock and are silted over. A large butterfly valve is at the base of the downstream gate. The valves regulated the water in and out of the lock. Next to the lock is a flat area at the base of the river bluff, which may have been the location of the lock keeper's residence. A large holding basin for canal boats was in front of the lock. It allowed them a place to wait their turn or spend the night. The next lock lowered the boats into a creek that empties into the river. It is mostly silted over, but some stone is still evident. The Rappahannock River Canal Company was never profitable, and by the 1850s it fell into disuse. Local farmers, including Lewis Ellis, kept sections operating for a while. In 1855 he agreed to do some repairs on the canal at his own expense. By the Civil War the canals were abandoned.[136]

Gold Mines

Not only was Ellis Ford impacted by the mills and canal system, it was also impacted by the many local gold mines in the area. The ford became a transportation route for the mines, and because the area around Ellis Ford was known as Mill Bank, the Mill Bank Mining Company was formed there. In July 1834, the Mill Bank Mining Company advertised in the Fredericksburg paper that the mines were in sight of Barnett's mill. Also, in 1834, Benjamin and Richard Barnett advertised 600 acres for sale in the gold belt.[137] As late as the 1850s, the mines were called "Mill Bank Mines."[138] A Union Civil War soldier recounts Ellis Ford's involvement in mining:

---

135 John Couty, *Rappahannock River Canal Improvements, 1845*, (Museum of Culpeper History, Culpeper, Va.).
136 Eugene M. Scheel, *Culpeper, A Virginia County's History Through 1920*, (Orange, Green Publishers, Inc., 1982), p. 149.
137 Ibid., p. 126.
138 Eugene M. Scheel, *The Historical Site Survey And Archaeological Reconnaissance of Culpeper County, Virginia, November 1992 - April 1994*. Richardsville. p. 12.

"Ellis Ford is in the center of the gold region of Virginia, and many works still remained which were formerly used obtaining that mineral. Mr. Ellis . . . was in his younger days extensively engaged in that business and made wealthy by it . . . On the south bank of the river was a indenture in the soil which he said marked the site of a former canal used by him in forwarding products from the gold mines and from his plantation, to the navigable waters of the Rappahannock."[139]

The early 1800s mines were put out of business because of the California gold rush, and then the Civil War, both of which robbed labor. In 1875, six years after Lewis Ellis died, the mines were reincorporated as the Ellis Gold Mining and Reduction Company. It boasted 310 acres, cabins, blacksmith shop, and five shafts.[140] The mines closed in the 1880s due to a series of accidents, one of which involved an operator's death. He fell from a bucket used to extract dirt and ore from a hundred-foot mine shaft. Later, in the late 1890s the mine briefly reopened. On November 25, 1898, the Culpeper Exponent reported, *"work on the Ellis Gold Mine will resume in spring."*[141] In January 1899, the Exponent reports, *"Mining interests are taking on a revival in Chinquepin Neck work has commenced at the Kelly Mine in Fauquier and Ellis Mine."*[142]

After Lewis Ellis died, the 310 acres around Ellis Mine were sold to a woman named Linden Kent. She married a man named White, and after he died, she transferred the property to her sister Letta Kent. Letta, in turn, left it to her father, Robert Kent. In 1889, he sold the property to Thomas Williams.[143] Ten years later Williams sold the 310 acres to the Pittsburg Mining and Milling Company.[144] The mining company sold the property to John Dunn in 1920.[145] Helen Dunn sold it to the Purcell Lumber Company in 1952.[146]

Located east of the 310 acres of the Ellis Mines were mines owned and operated by Charles and Samuel Urquhart. They were part of 1,400 acres that included several operating shafts. In 1891, the land and mines were sold to the Powhatan Mining Company. The Powhatan Mining Company was owned by Larman G. Johnson, who was also the mining company's superintendent. The company's president was D. L. King of Washington, D.C.[147]

Larman Johnson built a large commissary at the location of Rappahannock City. Rappahannock City was a failed developmental project that the Urquharts were involved with. The commissary contained an office, a laboratory, rooms for prospective investors, and a home for Johnson. It burned down just prior to 1906. The largest mines were next to the commissary, and the remaining shafts are huge. There is a long narrow ridge extending hundreds of feet from one of the shafts, which is actually the tailings dumped from the wheel barrels.

---

139 George K Collins,. *Memoirs of the 149th Regiment,* New York Volunteer Infantry, (Syracuse, 1891), pp. 176-177.
140 Eugene M. Scheel, *Culpeper, A Virginia County's History Through 1920,* (Orange, Green Publishers, Inc., 1982), p. 127.
141 The Culpeper Exponent, November 25, 1898, vol. 18, p. 2.
142 The Culpeper Exponent, January 6, 1899, vol. 19, p. 2.
143 Culpeper County Deed Book 23, p. 134.
144 Culpeper County Deed Book 31, p. 125.
145 Culpeper County Deed Book 65, p. 260.
146 Culpeper County Deed Book 133, p. 320.
147 Eugene M. Scheel, Culpeper, *A Virginia County's History Through 1920,* (Orange, Green Publishers. Inc., 1982), pp.129-130.

Nearby, down the hill from the commissary, was a stamping mill. It was located next to a creek that was dammed up to power the mill. A Powhatan Mining Company's map labels the creek as "Johnson's Creek."[148] The stamping mill crushed rock to extract the gold. Mercury was used to separate the gold from the crushed rock, or it was just picked out by hand.

In 1895, a post office was established at the commissary and it was called Marganna. Marganna was the combination of the names of Larman Johnson's two daughters, Margaret and Anna.[149] The Powhatan - Marganna Mines were eventually made obsolete because of production costs. A major problem with the mines was flooding. They usually encountered water at sixty feet.[150] The Alaska gold rush was also occurring at this time, diverting interest from the Virginia mines.

Larman Johnson then tried a residential development project. He formed "The Johnson Land Company" and advertised the subdivision as "Mannahannock Park." Lots were offered for $2.50, $5.00, and $10.00. It was marketed as potential fruit tree farms, and he even proposed building a fruit canning factory. Johnson set aside 150 acres for streets, schools, churches, and a park.[151] The project failed, and in 1905 the German Savings and Loan auctioned the land off to Thomas Williams, who sold it to the Pittsburg Mining Company. Larman Johnson died before 1905, because deed records show that Anna Johnson, Larman's widow, would not sign the papers to release the title. The savings and loan took her to court.[152] In 1906, the mining company sold the land to a man named Butzner, retaining the mining rights.[153] Butzner later sold it to Purcell Lumber Company.

Just prior to 1905, the Johnsons moved to a tract of land on the bluff above Snake Castle Dam. It was a 500 acre tract called Ellis Farm that Larman purchased from the Ellis heirs in 1890 for $500.[154] He had Burruss Walker, a local carpenter, build a house and called it West Marganna. When Anna died in 1913, she left the property to her daughters. One daughter, Anna, lived there and was said to have patrolled the property with horse, dog, and pistol. The house still stands, along with the outbuildings, cottages, and shop. It is presently owned by the Salvation Army.

The mines of Powhatan-Marganna Mining Company now appear as large gopher looking holes found throughout the area. The stamping mill's foundation is still evident next to Johnson Creek. Up the hill from the stamping mill, deep in the woods, is the stone foundation of the commissary, and lying next to the foundation, too heavy to be carried away, is the company's safe.

Rappahannock City

Prior to the Powhatan Mining Company obtaining the Urquharts' mines and surrounding land, a 170-acre developmental project called "Rappahannock City" was

---

148 Map of the Powhatan Mining Company.
149 Article of Margaret Johnson Martin.
150 Eugene M. Scheel, Culpeper, *A Virginia County's History Through 1920*, (Orange, Green Publishers, Inc., 1982), p. 130.
151 Brochure for The Johnson Land Company in possession of Fred Ricker.
152 Culpeper County Deed Book 37, pp 1-3.
153 Culpeper County Deed Book 38, p. 336.
154 Culpeper County Deed Book 24, p. 108.

attempted. In 1856, Charles Urquhart sold 170 acres of the 1400 acre tract to Julia and Ezra Bauder.[155] Julia was Charles Urquhart's wife's sister. The Bauders divided the land into streets and lots, with the pretense that gold may be on it. The lots were twenty five-hundred square foot for ten dollars each. Larger lots sold for thirty dollars.[156]

Charles Urquhart was a doctor who lived at Port Royal in Caroline County, which is downstream of Fredericksburg on the Rappahannock River. He was the doctor who treated, and pronounced dead, John Wilkes Booth. After Booth shot President Lincoln, his escape route took him through Port Royal, and pursuers trapped him in a nearby barn. They set it on fire and shot Booth in the neck. He was carried to the porch of the barn's owner, Richard Garret. A mattress was brought down for Booth and Dr. Urquhart was summoned from Port Royal to treat him. Urquhart determined that Booth could not survive a trip to Washington and attended him until he died. Upon his death, Dr. Urquhart cut off a lock of Booth's hair as a memento; unfortunately it was given away in the 1930's and lost.[157]

In July of 1866, Dr. Charles Urquhart was visiting Julia and Ezra Bauder at Rappahannock City when he had a stroke and died. He may have been a partner in the developmental project, and that may be the reason for his visit. Dr. Urquhart is buried, as requested, in the family graveyard, which is now next to Germanna Community College. That is where he was raised by his parents, who operated a mill there. The inscription on the grave marker reads, "*He now reposes by the side of his mother, his ashes will mingle with his kindred, whilst the sod which he trod in his infancy covers his remains.*"[158]

Ezra Bauder, known as professor Bauder, became the principle of the elementary school at Brandy Station in 1872. Four years later he became the headmaster of the Brandy Station Wheatley Academy.[159] The 1870 tax records show that Ezra owned 1400 acres. He may have inherited the rest of Charles Urquhart's property after his death. Nevertheless, Ezra lost the 170 acres in 1876 for non payment of taxes. By 1890, he was living in Laurinburg, North Carolina.[160]

In 1876, W. D. Foster purchased the 170 acres of Rappahannock City from the County Treasurer for $85.00. Foster requested that 79 acres of the 170 acres be set aside for Ezra Bauder. He kept the remaining 91 acres. The deed records documenting the transaction, and an accompanying survey, confirms it as the location of Rappahannock City.[161]

Tax records of 1880 show Ezra as owning 75 acres with 5 acres of it improved. The 1880 tax records also show Charles Urquhart's brother and sister-in-law, Samuel and Louisa, as owning 1230 acres, 1220 of them unimproved. The records have a question mark next to their name, indicating that it was not certain if they owned the land. In any event, ten years later Louisa sold the land to Larman Johnson and the Powhatan Mining Company. The 170 acres of Rappahannock City were also sold at that time and it became the location of Johnson's home and commissary.[162]

---

155 Culpeper County Deed Book 18, pp. 342-343.
156 Town and Country, Free Lance-Star, February 5, 2005, pp. 5, 6, 11.
157 Ibid., p. 6.
158 Carrol M. Garnett, *Fort Lowry and Raiders On The Rappahannock*, (New York, Vantage Press, 2002), p. 233.
159 Ibid., p. 6.
160 Culpeper County Deed Book 23, p. 503.
161 Culpeper County Deed Book 18, pp. 339-343.
162 Culpeper County Deed Book 23, pp. 486-488, 503.

The war, reconstruction, and lean years prevented Rappahannock City to ever materialize, and only a few houses were ever built. The last residents were the John Minor Smith family, who probably lived in Bauder's house. They moved away in the 1920s.[163] The old timers around Richardsville later referred to the area as *"the city field."*[164]

Civil War

Ellis Ford is very well documented in the Civil War records. In Official War Records, or individual soldier accounts, it is called either Ellis, or its older name, Barnetts Ford. The location and quality as a crossing made the ford a contested and guarded site. Records as early as May 1862 indicate Ellis Ford was of military importance, and from then on, the ford was heavily used and fought over until spring of 1864. At that time, the contesting armies vacated the area and moved toward Richmond.

1862

Ellis Ford first emerges in May of 1862 when Union troops stationed across the Rappahannock River at Fredericksburg sent a reconnaissance along the north side of the river. The Official Records state that they, *"struck the river at Ellis' Mill."*[165] Later that month, when Stonewall Jackson was implementing his famed Valley Campaign, Union troops were sent to the Shenandoah Valley from the Fredericksburg area. In the process of the transfer they needed to secure the fords. A soldier from the 9th Massachusetts Volunteer Infantry wrote:

"Our 1st division was ordered to hold the fords on the Rappahannock river, and prevent the enemy from crossing. The division was furnished with a supply train and intrenching implements and it was accompanied by two batteries of artillery . . . The regiment bivouacked at Hartwood Church on the night of the 28th, and near the Rappahannock on the night of the 29th. On the 30th we encamped in a belt of woods on the bank of the river, in the vicinity of Ellis Ford. Our pickets were posted along the river. We found the enemy's pickets on duty on the opposite bank. Our fatigue party dug rifle pits and threw up intrenchments. On the night of June 2, while engaged in work on the rifle pit near the ford, the enemy opened fire from a piece of artillery with grapeshot. They fortunately fired too high to kill, and our men escaped injury."[166]

There is a two hundred-foot trench line on the ridge north of Ellis's Mill. It lies above a stone wall, which was probably an edge to an old road. The Confederate cannon on the south side of the river may have been fired from a flattened spot on the bluff.

Later that summer Ellis Ford was again used by Union forces. Most reports at this time refer to the crossing as Barnetts Ford. On July 12, 1862, when General Pope crossed the Rappahannock River and entered Culpeper County, he established strong

---

163 Interview with Fred Ricker, Lewis Ellis descendant and Richardsville resident.
164 Eugene M. Scheel, *The Historical Site Survey And Archaeological Reconnaissance of Culpeper County, Virginia*, November 1992 - April 1994. Richardsville, p. 15.
165 O.R., vol. 12, pt. 1, p. 161.
166 Daniel George McNamara, *The History of the Ninth Regiment Massachusetts Volunteer Infantry*, (Boston, 1899), p. 307.

pickets on the river as far as Fredericksburg. On July 28, the 6th New York Cavalry, consisting of eight companies, was sent to establish a camp at Ellis Ford. They sent out patrols across the river on the roads leading to Orange.

Contrary to Pope's reputation of abusing local citizens, orders were strict to the 6th New York. The commander, Colonel Thomas Devin was instructed, "*In procurement of supplies from the country it must be done in the mode pointed out in orders, not in indiscriminate marauding by soldiers. Keep your men from strolling about the neighborhood of your camp. For this purpose have a guard posted, and never allow a horse to be taken from a picket-rope except to go on some duty.*"[167]

On August 18, after the Battle of Cedar Mountain, Pope issued orders for the army to withdraw to the north side of the Rappahannock in three columns. One column crossed at Ellis (Barnetts) and Kellys Ford, one column crossed at Rappahannock Station, and the third crossed at Sulphur Springs.[168] He then fortified the northern bank to await Lee.

During Pope's retreat, the Confederate cavalry engaged the Union forces. A member of the famed Black Horse Cavalry recalls, "*The fourth regiment crossed the Rappahannock River at Wallis ford, and marching through farms, regardless of the roads, came into the main road from Culpeper Court house to Fredericksburg, and turning to the right, attacked the cavalry protecting Popes extreme left and drove it across the Rappahannock at Ellis Ford.*"[169]

By August 19, the retreating columns were on the other side of the river. As Pope's army retreated across Ellis Ford, they left, as Union General F. J. Porter describes, "*much property*," because of the lack of wagons.[170] Also at Ellis Ford, a Union division under Brigadier General Stevens began to entrench, even though his request for entrenching tools was not fulfilled. The next day Steven's Division proceeded to Kellys Ford, and Ellis Ford was then guarded by cavalry belonging to Brigadier General Buford's brigade. It was a regiment from his brigade covering the ford as he proceeded with the rest of his brigade to Kellys Ford. Buford covered the major intersections and protected the infantry's front as they established themselves on the north side of the river.[171]

The day before, on August 18, Major General Burnside, who was opposite Fredericksburg at Falmouth, was ordered to send reinforcements to Ellis Ford and entrench.[172] But it was not until August 22 that troops were sent. They belonged to Major General Morrel's Division of 5th Corps, and were part of the first reinforcements sent to Pope from McClellan's army.[173] When Morrel arrived in Fredericksburg he was ordered to Ellis Ford and immediately sent Brigadier General Griffin's brigade, the 6th New York Cavalry, Colonel Brodhead 1st Michigan Cavalry, and a section of artillery.

By August 24, Morrel's entire division was at Ellis Ford. The next day, along with the rest of the Corps, they were ordered northwest. Morrel left Griffin's brigade of

---

167 O.R., vol. 12, pt. 3, p. 515.
168 Ibid., p. 598.
169 John Scott, *The Black Horse Cavalry*, in the Philadelphia Weekly Times, 1879.
170 O.R., vol. 12, pt. 2 supplement, p. 919.
171 O.R., vol. 51, pp. 748-749.
172 O.R., vol. 12, pt. 3, p. 593.
173 Ibid., p. 621.

infantry, along with an artillery battery, at Ellis Ford.[174] The movement was in response to Pope observing Stonewall Jackson's entire army moving to his right. Pope was nervous because two days earlier, on August 22, the Confederate cavalry under Jeb Stuart, circled around to his rear at Catlett's Station and captured his headquarters, including his coat. Even so, on August 27, Jackson's Army was in Popes rear at Manassas. The Rappahannock River, including Ellis Ford, was abandoned as Pope raced to stop Jackson.

The Battle of Second Manassas followed and Pope was driven back to Washington. Colonel Brodhead, commander of the First Michigan Cavalry, who was stationed at Ellis Ford afew days earlier, was killed during the battle.[175] After Lee's invasion of Maryland failed, and he retreated back to Virginia, the Union army under George McClellan slowly followed. At Warrenton McClellan stopped, and his troops immediately plundered the countryside. On November 7, McClellan was replaced by General Burnside because of the lethargic pursuit.

Within a week Burnside began to transfer troops from Warrenton to Fredericksburg. In the process, the fords of the Rappahannock again became important. On the north side of the river, Union pickets were placed at various locations on the roads leading to Ellis, Kempers, and Kellys Ford. At Ellis Ford itself, the picket was a squadron of the 8th Pennsylvania Cavalry. A post of twenty-five men was kept at the intersection of the road leading to Ellis Ford at Pine View. The Confederates were not picketing the ford in force yet. On November 21, the commanding Union officer, Colonel Duffie, reported, *"The river can, with some difficulty, be forded by cavalry, but not artillery. The officer in command at Ellis Ford was very confident that there was no force of enemy near there, as he crossed today, and their pickets disappeared; returning, however, when he recrossed, though very cautiously."*[176] It had been raining for three days.

As both armies raced to Fredericksburg, things started heating up in the Ellis Ford area. On November 28, a Confederate raiding party, some 700 to 800 strong, crossed the Rappahannock and attacked the 3rd Pennsylvania Cavalry at Hartwood Church. The Pennsylvania troopers were under the command of Captain Johnson. The raiding party approached through the woods, staying off the roads, and took them by surprise. More than 80 Union soldiers were captured, along with their horses and equipment. The Confederates then returned to the south bank of the Rappahannock, via Ellis Ford. Burnside was so infuriated that he wired Lincoln and requested that Johnson be relieved of command.[177]

By December, both armies settled in at Fredericksburg, with the Union army on the north bank and Lee's army on the south bank. General Burnside ordered all the fords across the Rappahannock guarded to prevent a surprise attack. On December 1, he sent out two cavalry regiments under Brigadier General W. W. Averell. They went up the north side of the Rappahannock River, all the way to Ellis Ford. The purpose of the reconnaissance was to examine all the fords and the roads to them. Averell reported back that, *"I was above Ellis Ford, and one of my officers and some of my men, who had been there, described the crossing as deep and uncertain."*[178]

After the Battle of Fredericksburg on December 13, Burnside continued to hold

---

174   O.R., vol. 51, p. 761.
175   Mark M. Boatner, III, *The Civil War Dictionary,* (New York, David McKay Company, Inc., 1959), pp. 88, 797.
176   O.R., vol. 21, p. 782.
177   Ibid., pp. 13-14.
178   Ibid., p. 21.

the fords along the river and send out scouting parties. On one of these scouting parties, the 6th New York Cavalry used Ellis Ford to dash across and reconnoiter.[179] The scouting parties convinced the Confederates that the fords needed better protection. On December 25, Union scouts reported that the Confederates strengthened their picket at Ellis Ford and added three pieces of artillery.

The Confederates also sent scouting parties across the river near Ellis Ford. Union commander, Brigadier General Averell of the 1st Cavalry Brigade, reports, *"Scouts are sent over every few hours, who approach our lines and return. Five came over whilst my scout was hidden in the vicinity of Ellis Ford."*[180]

Not only did scouting parties cross at Ellis Ford, large forces of Union troops crossed too. A Confederate's report states that, *"About December 30, a portion of Sigel's corps crossed the Rappahannock at Ellis Ford and returned by the same route to Stafford on the next day without accomplishing any damage to us."*[181] This was Union Colonel Barnes 1st Division of the 5th Corps, which had crossed earlier that day at Richards Ford. As previously explained in the chapter on Richards Ford, on December 30, 1862, as a diversionary action, Barnes crossed the river and marched to Ellis Ford.

1863

Throughout January the fords along the river were used for raiding parties, scouts, and deserters. The deserters in the area were mostly part of Burnside's army. After Burnside's ill fated "Mud March," the deserters were so numerous that local farmers came into Union lines complaining of the horrors committed and asked for protection.[182]

Scouting and raiding parties were frequent. On January 26, a Confederate raiding party of three hundred men crossed into Fauquier County at Kellys Ford and ran into a Union scouting party. After skirmishing with them, the Confederates recrossed the river at Ellis Ford, leaving casualties behind. The commander of the Union cavalry, Colonel Cesnola, describes the raid, *"I sent 50 men, under Captain Parnell, in pursuit of them as soon as I heard it, and he traced them as far as Ellis Ford, from which they had already recrossed. Three rebel bodies were also reported lying in the woods, and some wounded rebels. I sent a doctor expressly there to see and attend to them."*[183]

Because of the threat of being flanked from the upstream river fords, Lee kept men posted at Ellis Ford. The fords were obstructed with iron and wire, which were meant to entangle horses while sharpshooters picked off their riders.[184] The flanking movement Lee suspected eventually occurred in late April when General Hooker, now in command of the Union army, began the Chancellorsville campaign. On April 28, 1863, during the march along the north side of the river, Union Colonel Devin reported, *"made a reconnaissance in person (after halting and feeding horses and men) to Ellis Ford. Woke up their infantry, who came down into the rifle pits and drew a bead on us. They sent one shot at*

---

179 City of Fredericksburg, Virginia, *Historic Resources Along the Rappahannock and Rapidan Rivers*, (Fredericksburg, Va., Billingley Printing and Engraving, 2002), p. 129.
180 O.R., vol. 21, pp. 782
181 Ibid., p. 734.
182 Ibid., p. 757.
183 Ibid., p. 758.
184 O.R. vol. 25, pt. 2, p. 276.

a picket I left . . . Picketed near Ellis, Kemper, and Fields . . ."[185] Ellis Ford was ultimately secured by Union forces from the other side of the river when Meade's 5th Corps marched through nearby Richardsville. At that time detachments of the 8th Pennsylvania Cavalry were sent to Ellis and Richards Ford. They found no Confederates at Ellis Ford, however, twenty-nine Confederate soldiers were surprised and captured at Richards Ford.[186]

Later in May, after Chancellorsville, the Union army was aware that the Confederates were preparing to move. They were concerned that Lee would cross the river and attack them, but they did not know where. In response to the threat, all the fords, ferries, dams, and other crossings in the area were guarded.[187] On May 28, two regiments belonging to the Union Fifth Corps, under Major General George Meade, were ordered to Ellis Ford. A battery was also ordered there. By May 31, the two regiments of Union soldiers, including the battery, were on the north side of the ford.[188]

Lee was not planning to cross the river and attack. His plans were far more grandiose. He planned to invade the north. To do this, he needed to screen his troop movements. A major part of this screening action occurred on June 9 with the Battle of Brandy Station. It was the largest cavalry battle of the war, and Confederate General Jeb Stuart was able to prevent the detection of Lee's troop movements. During this battle the Confederate picket was removed from Ellis Ford, but not before a deserter from the 63rd North Carolina Cavalry came across the river. He reported, *"a squadron of his regiment picketed at Ellis; believes there is a large force of infantry and cavalry back, but not sure; says his regiment has only arrived two weeks since from North Carolina."*[189]

After Lee's invasion was stopped at Gettysburg, and he retreated to the south side of the Rappahannock, Union scouts reported Longstreet's Corps and Stuart's cavalry were at Culpeper, and all the river fords were guarded. They also reported that the Confederates drove a herd of cattle across the river at Ellis Ford.[190] By the end of July, Union pickets were on the north side of the Rappahannock from Waterloo to Ellis Ford.

To find out more about Lee, and whether to continue moving south, Meade decided to send a reconnaissance in force into Culpeper County. On August 1, 1863, he sent three cavalry divisions, supported by two infantry corps, across the river from Rappahannock Station. The result was the Second Battle of Brandy Station. The 1st Cavalry Division, under General Buford, drove the Confederates toward Culpeper until they were stopped at Inlet, just northeast of town.

Ellis Ford was considered as a crossing point during this probe. A report on August 1 states, *"found the ford high and impassable to infantry. One large flat-boat, used as a ferry, was sunk by my orders and a small boat removed and placed under guard. The mill commanding the ford I find to have been loopholed for musketry and strengthened with railroad iron. A rifle pit is also dug on the hill above the mill. These preparations for defense made by our troops last spring. No enemy has been seen at this point since our arrival. One horse man and two armed men of the rebel crossed yesterday to this side by boat, and our still on this side."* [191]

---

185 Ibid., p. 276.
186 O.R., vol. 25, pt. 1, pp. 506, 1079.
187 O.R., vol. 25, pt. 2, p. 535.
188 Ibid., p. 572.
189 O.R., vol. 27, pt. 3, p. 39.
190 Ibid., p. 782.
191 Ibid., p. 822.

The ford was still unpassable on August 5, Colonel Thomas Devin, 1st Brigade, 2nd Cavalry Division reported, "*I have the honor to state that the party I sent to Barnett's Ford have returned.*" *They were unable to cross, as the Rappahannock was not fordable at that point.*"[192] Devin used the older name, Barnetts Ford.

The reconnaissance convinced Meade that Lee was in force in Culpeper County, so he chose to dig in along the north bank of the Rappahannock. Centered around Rappahannock Station, Meade posted infantry troops as far downstream as Ellis Ford. Cavalry picketed the river from Ellis Ford to U. S. Mine Ford.[193] Later the 2nd Corps replaced the cavalry.[194]

The soldiers assigned to Ellis Ford were the 102nd New York Infantry, part of the same brigade that guarded Skinkers Ford. They arrived there on August 3, and found the ford impassable due to high water. The 102nd was under strength because of defending Culp's Hill at Gettysburg, but their morale was high. Their division commander, General Greene, located his headquarters near Ellis Ford and stationed a picket of fifty men at the ford itself. He also stationed soldiers at Kempers Ford, a mile and a half upstream, and at Skinkers Ford, a mile and a half downstream.

Greene placed the bulk of the brigade that the 102nd belonged to behind the first ridge of hills away from Ellis Ford, out of sight.[195] They remained there until September 20. Among these soldiers was a private by the name of Morris Bartlett, belonging to 102nd New York Infantry. His letters home reveal what was occurring there at that time. Bartlett's first letter written from Ellis Ford was on July 30, 1863. He writes to his parents in Italy, New York:

"We are hear and the rebels are across the river. Our cavalry went to reconoiter yesterday but their ford was to strong to think of undertaking to cross so our cavalry came back but we are watching them and they will have to keep their eyes open or they might get a bug in their ear. Reports say that they have been reinforced to quite an extent, how true it is I am not supposed to know. The army is in very good condition taking into consideration they have marched over 500 miles, fought a heavy battle, been on short rations. A few days rest and enough to eat will bring us all right again and when we are filed up to 1040 men to a regt. The rebs had better look sharp."[196]

As indicated, the Union soldiers were in good spirts, and confident after their victory at Gettysburg. Bartlett, although, reveals that the brigade numbered around 1,000 men, only regimental strength. He writes, "*The cars are bringing up supplies as fast as they can, and this is where the whole army draws its supplies.*" The cars he refers to are from the Orange and Alexandria Railroad, which were unloading supplies at the Bealeton depot.[197] Dry wood must have been a problem because he goes on to say, "*Wood and water is very scarce hear. The quartermaster draws their wood but we have to get our water wherever we can, sometimes go 2 miles after it and very poor at that.*" Bartlett describes the weather when he writes, "*The weather is quite warm with showers once on a while. There is not much grain in this part of the country but grass in plenty good foraging for the horses.*"

192 O.R., vol. 29, pt. 2, p. 6.
193 Ibid., p. 62.
194 Ibid., p. 77.
195 O.R., vol 27, pt. 3, p. 829.
196 Letters of Morris Bartlett, Co. H, 102 NY Infantry.
197 O.R., vol. 27, pt. 3, p. 783.

On August 6, Bartlett writes another letter home and describes the hardships that were going on in the area: *"Well the news is very scarce there is non of any consequence only the 6th New York Cavalry crossed at Kellys Ford yesterday morning and scouted to the Rapidan down as far as hear and crossed back last night. The rebels got the wind of their coming and quietly skedaddled."* He continues, *"I was a party of 10 men that went out with the quartermaster after hay yesterday. We went three miles and took all the hay a local farmer had cut . . . The farmer complained that he and his niggers would starve to death. He said that all he had to live on for the last 4 weeks was hard tack and rye coffee without sugar in it . . . There is not much growing in this part of Virginia this season there is no one to take care of it."*[198]

This shows how desolate the local area was due to the war, but for Bartlett things were different; they received abundant supplies: *"there has been no trouble with short rations. We got fresh bread yesterday today we have drawn rice, molasses, dried apples fresh beef, coffee, sugar, desecated vegetables, soap, salt and candles. We have pork and soft bread today I believe."* Bartlett also tells how he spends the time, *"We lay either in our tents or in the woods. We go on picket once 4 days we go on by Regt. And once in 4 days we act as a reserve."*[199]

Bartlett's next letter further describes the local conditions. The residents were all but starving and he was concerned how they were going to survive. Bartlett writes, *"The citizens of VA. are in a starving condition they have nothing to eat except what they get from the army. Well I don't know how they will live when the Army gets away."*[200]

Bartlett continued to picket Ellis Ford the rest of August through mid September. They evidently became cordial with the Confederate pickets on the other side of the river. In a letter dated August 19, Bartlett writes, *"The rebel pickets are just across the river not over 20 rods from us. We often yell over at them some question and generally give us some answer."* By September, they were doing some trading. On September 2 he writes, *"I was on picket yesterday I was just opposite a picket post of the Rebs they came down to the river and wanted to exchange papers. We did not have any to exchange and even if we would not be allowed to do it. We sit in site of each other in easy rifle range but we don't fire at each other."*

The weather started cooling down in September and it must have been exceptionally cold. Bartlett writes about the weather, *"quite cool now the nights are very cold, much colder than in New York State . . ."* Interestingly, he goes on to write about the cost of obtaining a warm blanket and overcoat. Evidently he had to buy them if he threw the ones issued away. He writes, *"a man can sleep comfortably under a wool blanket which I have not got and don't believe I shall get one yet in a month for if I do get one then have to go on a march I should throw it away and there would go $3.50 and I should have to draw another one ditto overcoat."*

On September 1, Bartlett describes the incident previously mentioned in the Skinkers Ford chapter, that is, when the Confederate guerrillas crossed the dam in the night and killed a Union picket. Bartlett describes the event, *"The camp was thrown in quite an excitement last night some Bushwackers I guess fired on our pickets and the news*

---

198 Letters of Morris Bartlett, Co. H, 102 NY Infantry.
199 Ibid.
200 Ibid.

was that the Rebs were going to cross below the Ford. The 149th NY was thrown forward as skirmishers but there was no attempt made by the Rebs to cross."

Lee had previously withdrawn from the Rappahannock to the south bank of the Rapidan on August 9, but as indicated, the guerillas were still active around Ellis Ford. The Rapidan was a more defensible position and the troops could be better supplied. Lee did, however, leave his cavalry in Culpeper County. They continued to picket the fords and keep an eye on Meade until September 13, when Union cavalry crossed the Rappahannock and entered Culpeper. The Union army followed the next day. By September 22, Bartlett was opposite the Rapidan at Raccoon Ford.

On September 8, Lee sent Longstreet's Corps to Tennessee to reinforce General Bragg. The result was the Confederate victory of Chickamauga. In response, on September 24, against Meade's wishes, Lincoln dispatched the 11th and 12th Corps Tennessee. Morris Bartlett, belonging to the 12th, went with them, and unfortunately, died there.

The departure of Meade to the Rapidan offered some peacefulness for Ellis Ford, although, it did not last long. With the absence of the 11th and 12th Corps, Lee launched a campaign driving into Northern Virginia, attacking Meade in a flanking maneuver, and threatening Washington. It began on October 10, when Lee crossed back into Culpeper County and began a series of flanking marches. Staying on the defensive, Meade retreated back toward Washington. On October 14, Lee caught up to him at Bristoe Station and suffered a costly repulse by a disastrous charge ordered by A.P. Hill. Meade then dug in at Centerville in a position too strong to attack. With his supply lines stretched, Lee decided to retire back to the south bank of the Rappahannock, tearing up the railroad along the way. Meade followed, and once again, they faced each other across the Rappahannock.

Lee maintained a bridgehead at Rappahannock Station. At Kellys Ford he stationed Ewell's Corps. On November 7, in a coordinated effort, Meade attacked Lee's bridgehead at Rappahannock Station and forced a crossing at Kellys Ford. He also ordered cavalry to cross at Ellis and Kempers Fords. Brigadier General Kilpatrick states, *"My people are at Ellis Ford and have only seen a small force of cavalry . . . I shall be at Ellis Ford ready to cross at an early hour."*[201] In the uncharacteristic evening attack at Rappahannock Station, Meade caught Lee off guard. Lee's troops were driven back across the river with a loss of 1,400 men. He lost another 400 men earlier in the day when two of Meade's Corps crossed at Kellys Ford.

With the loss of the bridgehead, and with Union troops across at Kellys Ford, Lee retreated back to Rapidan. There he remained, dug in on the south side of the river until spring. Meade occupied Culpeper County and made Brandy Station his base of operations. With his back to the Rappahannock, it was essential to guard all the fords, including Ellis. This time, however, he had to guard it from the south bank.

In late November, as things started heating up in the Mine Run Campaign, Ellis Ford became important again. In preparation for the campaign, Union cavalry at Morrisville was sent to secure the fords on the Rapidan River and protect the Union left flank during the infantry movements. To get to the Rapidan they had to first cross the Rappahannock.

On November 23, 3,000 cavalry troopers of the 2nd Division, under Brigadier General Gregg, crossed at Ellis Ford.[202] That evening he reported, *"The advance of my*

---
201 O.R., vol. 29, pt. 2, p. 432.
202 Ibid., p. 480.

Div had crossed the Rapidan at Eley's Ford before I received order countermarching a movement for today. There are 7 cavalryman on picket on the other side. Only one regt. was seen by the enemy. I now have a Brig at Richardsville and one near Ellis Ford. I have sent my wagon train to Brandy Station to load forage. A party of 30 Rebel Cav was at Richardsville this morning. My headquarters near Ellis Ford."[203]

A Union soldier from the 1st Maine Cavalry had the following account of the crossing, *"On the twenty fourth of November a forward movement of the whole army was commenced, with the intention of trying once more to whip the rebel forces before going in to winter quarters . . . The first Maine crossed the Rappahannock at Ellis Ford, and marching to the Rapidan, a portion stood picket that night and the next day at Ely's Ford, while the rest went into camp near Richardsville. On the twenty-sixth the Rapidan was crossed, and the division took the left of the army."*[204]

After the Mine Run Campaign, and like the other fords downstream, Ellis Ford was picketed throughout the winter. On December 3, Brigadier General Gregg of the 2nd Cavalry Division reported, *"Nothing remains at Richardsville but troops of my division . . . Some of the enemy's cavalry were seen opposite Ellis Ford yesterday. I suppose they were guerrilla scouts."*[205] The next day, Gregg wrote the following report, *"One brigade is posted at Sheppard's Grove Post Office . . . The other brigade is at Richardsville picketing the lower fords and the Rappahannock."*[206] This would have definitely included Ellis Ford.

Gregg's 2nd Division was moved across the Rappahannock River to Morrisville, and troopers from the 3rd Division, under Kilpatrick, were assigned to Ellis Ford. They were the same troopers mentioned in the previous chapters on Richards and Skinkers Fords, those belonging to Brigadier General Henry Davies 1st Brigade. Davies sent a report on January 12, 1864, *"The command is doing picket duty on the extreme left and front of the Army. The vedettes stretching from Germanna on the Rapidan across the neck to Kempers dam on the Rappahannock patrolling the roads to Ellis and Elys Fords."*[207]

1864

The congenial relationships with the enemy pickets that Morris Bartlett wrote of in 1863 were gone in 1864. It was dangerous duty to patrol and picket the fords. The fords were isolated and the roads offered chances for ambush. Official Reports from January alone document three ambushes on the road to Ellis Ford from Richardsville. On January 12, 1864, Davies reports, *"the patrol of 6 men were attacked by concealed guerillas in a dense pine woods and 5 captured."* On January 17, he reports, *"The patrol of 1 Sergeant and 7 men returning from Ellis Ford were surrounded by the enemy in ambuscade and 7 men captured . . ."* On January 22, he reports, *"The patrol of 1 commissioned and 30 men were attacked going to Ellis Ford by a party of men in ambush. Loss 1 man killed, 6 wounded and 4 captured."*[208]

---

203 Ibid., p. 479.
204 Edward P. Tobie, *History of the First Maine Cavalry, 1861-1865*, (Boston, 1887), p. 210.
205 O.R., vol., 29, pt., 2, p. 528.
206 Ibid., p. 528.
207 O.R., vol. 33, pp. 459-460.
208 Ibid., pp. 459-460.

Davies gave a detailed report of the January 22 ambush, "*Lieutenant Munson, Fifth New York Cavalry, with 30 men of the same regiment, left the reserve near Southard's Cross-roads at 2:30 p.m. yesterday, to patrol Ellis Ford. When within short distance of the ford and in dense woods they were suddenly fired upon from the rear on both sides of the road by from 60 - 70 dismounted men, most of them wearing the United States blue overcoats. Wheeling about, Lieutenant Munson with men charge, repulsing the enemy instantly and putting him into flight through the woods. Several of the rebels were wounded. We had 1 man killed and 4 wounded, besides 3 horses killed. Further pursuit was impossible on account of the thickness of the woods.*"[209]

To further illustrate how dangerous things got, J. Z. H. Scott, a Virginia cavalryman, describes a massacre of Union cavalry pickets at a ford eight miles downstream. He writes, "*I went down to Stafford - while the Yankees were fighting on the Spotsylvania side. On this expedition I reached the United States Ford where I had once done picket duty - the year before. The Yankees had a picket there, and with some dozen other scouts and whom I met in my wanderings it was agreed that we should cross the river in a boat and capture those pickets . . . three of four trips in the boat put us across. Each man had a double barreled shot gun charged with buckshot, and a pistol or two to boot, and we were confident of cleaning up our supposed three dozen adversaries before they got awake. Going well back into the hills - we went clear around the objects of our attack and approached them from above. We got into the bed of the old canal and quietly crept down until we were abreast of the picket camp - which was situated on a little plateau between the canal and the river . . . I being familiar with the ground - took one man and passed down beyond the camp to take possession of the road by which the Yankees would have to escape if they tried. It was agreed that the main body of our party would spring over the canal bank and rushing on the camp demand its surrender. If the surrender was made without firing, we would take them all prisoners and quietly cross the river again - but if a shot was fired we would kill them all. This was rendered necessary by the proximity of a cavalry camp up on the hill - and the difficulty anticipated in recrossing the river which was swollen . . . our men . . . leaped into the camp and called for surrender. No doubt all the Yankees would have complied and some of them did. But we had a cold blooded fellow by the name of R___ who had done service with General Walker in Nicaragua . . . He . . . killed the first Yankee he came to. Another remonstrated that the man had surrendered - whereupon R___ shot him also. A fusilade ensued in which all the Yankees except two were killed, but the whole party turned to be only thirteen . . . The sentinel tried to escape down the road I was guarding. I shot at him and he went down. Another Yankee came running down the same way. I fired my other barrel at him (and) he fell on his hands and knees. I drew my pistol but he was finished by some one else before I could use it.*"[210]

February and March appear to be quiet but the hardships continue. There were periods of extreme cold. On February 20, a Union cavalryman named Wilbur Fisk writes of the cold, "*We have had some severe cold weather here during the present week. I believe it has been the coldest that I have known in Virginia.*" Fisk had been fighting in

---

209 Ibid., p. 402.
210 City of Fredericksburg, Virginia, *Historic Resources Along the Rappahannock and Rapidan Rivers*, (Fredericksburg, Va., Billingley Printing and Engraving, 2002), p. 116.

Virginia for three years. He goes on to say, *"Canteens of water are sure to solid every night, and even in the day time they will freeze if left more than a yard and a half from the fire."* It was during this freezing weather that Fisk gets assigned three days picket duty.[211]

Fisk writes about the picket duty, *"we were divided . . . one half being sent to the reserve, and the other half was distributed to the different posts along the line . . . we spend half of the time there, and the other half on post, making thirty hours each. I found myself with those who were counted off to go on post the first twelve hours. There were three men on each post, one of whom was stationed several rods further out towards the enemy, all relieving each other every two hours."* During this time the soldiers were required to walk a "beat" and keep a sharp look out. Anything suspicious was reported to the corporal of the post, who relayed it to the commanding officer of the detail.[212]

The cold was so brutal that they built extremely hot fires. The fires were so hot they had to cover their faces to keep them from burning, but their backsides felt the opposite. Fisk writes, *"The wind made itself felt as much from the rear, as the fire did from the front. If some malicious fiend had been sponging my back with ice cold water the sensations could not have been less desirable."* He goes on to write, *"Occasionally the torture was varied. A gust of wind would rush around the other quarter, and blow a perfect avalanche of fire smoke and ashes all over us."*[213]

On March 17, a snow storm hits, and that night Fisk writes, *"It's a regular northeaster, and it beats through the tent . . . the tent makes a poorer defense against a snow storm than it used to against the rain, and I believe I never had the occasion to commend it to highly for doing its duty in that respect . . . it is near midnight, and my last ration of candles is nearly burned out. Taps beat long ago, and I have been violating the rules of the camp ever since . . . But the storm has kept raging, and I have kept writing . . . My tent mates are all asleep, and some of them are snoring strong dismal strains of sepulchral music, as I write. I have deliberately made up my mind to join them-here I am fast asleep."*[214]

In April, activity significantly increases. On April 17, a regimental report of the 10th New York Cavalry stationed at Morrisville states, *"One man (Henry Jerdon) Co D killed and 3 badly wounded in a skirmish with guerrillas near Ellis ford."* One of the wounded, S.D. Lawrence, died of his wounds on April 21.[215]

The cavalry pickets were showing strain by the end of April. In the Cavalry Corps there were 1,800 men without horses. Major General Phil Sheridan, who had replaced Major General Alfred Pleasanton as Cavalry Corps commander, reported that the remaining horses in his three divisions were in deplorable condition. He requested to have the cavalry pickets replaced by infantry so the horses could be rested and given forage. Sheridan also requested that the picket line be reduced to only a few prominent points and only a few cavalrymen placed at the Rappahannock River fords. Sheridan writes, *"It is better to occasionally lose a cavalryman scouting or outpost duty than to render so many horses so unserviceable by their hard labor."*[216]

---

211 Emil and Ruth Rosenblatt, *Hard Marching Every Day, The Civil War Letters of Private Wilbur Fisk, 1861 - 1865,* (Lawrence, Kansas, University Press of Kansas, 1992), p. 193.
212 Ibid., pp. 193-194.
213 Ibid., p. 194.
214 Ibid., pp. 203-204.
215 O.R., vol. 33, p. 1034.
216 Ibid., p. 909.

On April 23, Union headquarters ordered Major General Phil Sheridan to make ready to move and unite various cavalry units. The order stated, "... *a portion of General Wilsons Division not less than brigade be held ready to move to unite with Gregg or act in conjunction with him by crossing at the lower fords on the Rappahannock (Ellis Ford).*"[217] The next day, Brigadier General Wilson, who had replaced Kilpatrick as 3rd Division commander, reported to Sheridan, "*Telegram just received. Orders have been given too the detachment at Southard's Cross Roads to send a strong patrol to Ellis Ford twice a day . . . The party at Groove Church (Goldvien) has been notified that Ellis Ford will be visited by other patrols.*"[218] The patrols belonged to the 10th New York Cavalry.

This was all in preparation of the Wilderness Campaign. After the Union army left the area on its drive south, no more records are found concerning Ellis Ford in the Civil War.

Post Civil War

Ellis Ford continued to be used as a local crossing until bridges were built at Ely and Germanna Fords. Its use then subsided and locals do not recall the road or ford being used since the early's 1900s. The locks and canal remain, even though they were built almost two hundred years ago. The last known residence of the Staunton- Barnett house was a bachelor named Douglas Curtis, who lived there in the early 1900s. The house fell down shortly after but the barn stood until the 1920s.[219] All that is left are the stone foundations. The Staunton-Barnett's Mill has disappeared, with only a few stones scattered about, but Ellis-Embrey Mill's foundation and race still survive. Civil war trenches can still be seen above them. Rappahannock City, although never really materializing, had some remnants of buildings reported in mining records of the late 1800s.[220] Today, nothing of it remains. Ellis Ford, now only accessible by river, still has road traces on both sides of the river. On the road trace on the south side of the river, as it goes up the bluff, carved into a large beech tree, the ford name survives as "ELLES FORD."

---

217 Ibid., p. 952.
218 Ibid., p. 963.
219 Interview with Fred Ricker, Lewis Ellis descendant and Richardsville resident.
220 Eugene M. Scheel, *The Historical Site Survey And Archaeological Reconnaissance of Culpeper County, Virginia, November 1992 - April 1994,* Richardsville Quad. p. 15.

Chapter Five

Rogers/ Kempers Ford

Approximately three miles upstream of Ellis Ford, and eleven miles upstream of the confluence, was Rogers Ford. The name of this crossing is determined by which side of the river you are on. The Rogers lived on the Culpeper side, and the Kempers lived on the Fauquier side. Older documents identify the ford as Kempers, which indicates that it was the original name. By the Civil War both names are used. Presently, the name Rogers Ford is predominant.

The distance from Rogers Ford to the Rapidan River is only two miles, thus creating a narrow entrance to a finger of land between the two rivers called "The Neck." The crest of land is the original path that John Lederer used in 1670, and now it is part of Route 610.

The entrance to The Neck is easily identified because of a fire tower. The fire tower was placed there in the late 1930s, probably a Civilian Conservation Corps (CCC) project. It was built to protect the timber industry in the area. Even now most of the land in The Neck is owned by timber companies.

Indians

In the early 1930s, the Smithsonian sent David I. Bushnell, Jr. to conduct field investigations of the Indian tribes located on the Rappahannock River above Fredericksburg. Since the only recorded encounter with the Indians on the river was by John Smith in 1608, he had only limited knowledge to go on. From Bushnell's expedition, and his field research, he identified sites of the various Manahoac Indian villages. One of the larger Manahoac settlements found was at Rogers Ford. His findings were published in the Smithsonian's Miscellaneous Collections, October 9, 1935.

The south bank of Rogers Ford is open and flat. Even though the land had been heavily farmed and plowed over the years, Bushnell found arrowheads of black flint, quartz, quartzite. The Indians used the long arrowheads to shoot fish in the water. Captain John Smith wrote that Virginia Indians fished with a line tied to the arrow.[221] Also, at Rogers Ford Bushnell found many pottery fragments.

The pottery he found was made not only by Manahoacs, but also Algonquians. Algonquians were enemies of the Manahoacs, so the area was occupied at different times by different tribes. Bushnell believed the pottery findings indicate that Rogers Ford may have been occupied long before the Manahoacs, and the two occupation periods were possibly separated by centuries.[222]

Settlement

The earliest record of the ford is the 1814 Rappahannock River Canal Company map by Laozi Baldwin. He labels the location as Allen's Dam. The dam would have

---

221 David I. Bushnel, *The Manahoac Tribes In Virginia,* 1608, (Smithsonian Institution, Washington D.C., 1936), p. 1.
222 Ibid., pp. 28-31.

been for a mill because the canal company had not reached that far upstream yet. Next to Allen's property was the Rogers. It was 180 acres that originally belonged to William Richards of Richards Ford. In 1812, William gave it to his daughter Elizabeth who was married to Captain Thomas Humphreys of "Locust Hill." Locust Hill was located on the Rapidan River, a mile from the property, across the narrowest point of The Neck. In 1827, they sold the land to James Rodgers. At that time the Rogers spelled their name as "Rodgers." For the next 100 years the property remained in the Rogers family.[223]

In 1849, James divided the land into two 90 acre tracks. He in turn gave each of his sons, Welford and James F., one of the tracks.[224] When Welford died in 1889, he left his 90 acres to his son Willie F. Rodgers.[225] In 1893, James F. deeded the other track to Willie.[226] In 1922, Willie lost the 180 acres to the Federal Land Bank of Baltimore because of non payment of the mortgage.[227]

Canal System

The 1845 Rappahannock River Canal Company's map by John Couty labeled Rogers Ford as Kempers Ford. The map shows a dam 6.5 ft. high and 200 ft. long. It backed up the river all the way to Mountain Run, three miles upstream. On the north bank was a short canal, only 197 yards long, with a wooden lock. Nothing of the lock remains, although the canal is still evident.[228]

Road and Ford

Just below the dam was the ford. The road to the ford began at present day Route 610, near the fire tower. It passed by the Roger's house and descended to the river. Once across the river, the road went to the left, up the hill, across a creek, and tied into present day Rogers Ford Road in Fauquier County.

Civil War

As with the other downstream fords, Rogers Ford was used during the same events. The first time it was mentioned was in Official War Records of November 20, 1862, just prior to the Battle of Fredericksburg. Brigadier General Pleasonton, commanding the Union Army's Cavalry Division reported, "*my pickets are now as high as Kemper's Ford.*"[229] In all military reports the name Kempers Ford is used.

Pleasonton was screening and picketing for Burnside while he was moving the entire army from Warrenton to Fredericksburg. Pleasonton also stated that, "*Their pickets are observed at the different fords on the opposite side.*" The opposite side included Culpeper

---

223 Culpeper County Deed Book FF, p. 349.
224 Culpeper County Deed Book 9, p. 369.
225 Culpeper County Will Book 3, p. 100.
226 Culpeper County Deed Book 26, p. 16.
227 Culpeper County Deed Book 79, p. 447.
228 John Couty, *Rappahannock River Canal Improvements, 1845*, (Museum of Culpeper History, Culpeper, Va.).
229 OR, vol. 21, pt. 1, p. 776.

County. He also makes an interesting observation about the local people. Pleasonton reported that there are two types of people, the poor and the aristocratic wealthy. The poor ones are very bitter against the wealthy and blame them for bringing on the war. He writes the poor, *"are always willing to show where the rich ones have hid their grain, fodder and horses."*[230]

Rogers Ford was picketed by the Confederates until the Gettysburg campaign. On June 6, 1863, just prior to Lee moving his army to Pennsylvania, Major General Meade, then in charge of the 5th Corps, received a report from one of his division commanders. It states, *"that at Kempers Ford the pickets yesterday were weak and few appeared. This morning they are stronger and show themselves in considerable numbers."*[231] Lee was screening his army as he prepared to move. Not until after Lee's invasion, and his retreat to Culpeper from Gettysburg, did the ford become important again. When the Union army followed Lee, and reached the Rappahannock River in early August, they posted the 137th New York, under Colonel Ireland, at Rogers Ford. The 137th was part of Greene's 3rd Brigade, the same brigade that was assigned to Ellis and Skinkers Ford. The 137th had their camp near the Kemper's house.[232]

Also, posted near Kempers Ford was the 109th and 111th Pennsylvania Volunteers. On August 3, a report from the division commander, Brigadier General Geary, states, *"Their regimental camps are concealed as far as practicable, and the regimental commanders are ordered to keep strict watch for any movement of the enemy."* The report also states that no Confederates have been seen across the river.[233]

The next day, however, General Greene reported about a dozen Confederate cavalry troopers across the river near Kempers Ford. He also reported two enemy regiments about a quarter mile from the ford. Colonel Ireland had his 137th regiment construct rifle pits commanding the ford and, *"a large work, capable of containing his whole command, about a hundred yards to the rear."*[234] They remained there until late September and then were transferred to Tennessee.

Rogers Ford remained quiet until November 7, 1863. At that time, Union cavalry under General Kilpatrick was instructed to cross at the ford while the rest of the Union army forced a crossing at Rappahannock Station and Kellys Ford. Once they were across the river, Lee retreated to the south side of the Rapidan River, where he remained until the following spring.

A couple of months after Lee retreated, just prior to the Mine Run Campaign, Union cavalry under Colonel Duffie reconnoitered Rogers Ford. He reported, *"that three squadrons of the Eight Pennsylvania Cavalry picketed Ellis and Kempers Fords and the road to Morrisville."* He also said that the river can be forded with cavalry but not artillery.[235]

After the Mine Run Campaign, Roger's Ford was continually picketed until spring of 1864. The pickets were the same as Ellis and Skinkers Ford, those belonging to Brigadier General Henry Davies 1st Brigade. They remained there until the Wilderness Campaign.

---

230 Ibid., p. 776.
231 OR, vol. 51, pt. 1, p. 1065.
232 OR, vol. 27, pt. 3, p. 860.
233 OR, vol. 21, pt. 3, p. 833.
234 Ibid
235 Ibid

Post Civil War

The name Rogers Ford became dominant after the Civil War. After Willie Rogers lost the property to the bank in 1922, it was sold to Harold Marean. At that time the land was bordered by Joseph Fields and George Kemper. The bank financed the property and Marean paid it off in 1927. In 1950, the property was sold to Basal Burke. The property changed ownership several more times until it ended up with the present owners, Gordon and Patricia Leary. Across the river, on the Kempers side, the land is owned by the Pucketts, and they operate the Rogers Ford Winery there.

Now, because the road to the ford is on private property, the only access to Rogers Ford is by river. The river banks are steep and show no sign of the crossing, however, remnants of the dam and canal are still evident. Just below the remnants of the dam, in the middle of the river, is a rock that was used to judge water depth before using the ford.

Epilogue

Fortunately for a region so rich in history, the majority of it remains unspoiled. The fords have returned to a natural state and the roads to the fords are mere traces. The Richards', Bell's, Pemberton's, Martin's, and Ellis's farms are grown over, but deep in the woods you can still find their house sites. The gold mines are long gone, yet remnants of shafts and stamp mills exist. Even though the canal system never panned out, the stone work for the most part endures, and is impressive 200 years later. Local names, such as Ellis Mine, Richards Ferry, and Snake Castle survive, while others, such as Oak Shade, Horseshoe, and Rappahannock City have been lost in time.

The river remains the same, and standing there, if you look hard enough, and use your imagination, you can see Amaroleck fishing upstream on the rocks. He uses a bow with a hemp string attached to the arrow. You can also imagine John Lederer, splashing across with horses, mules, Indian guides, and plenty of whiskey. Canal boats can be seen waiting for their turn to go through the lock, while the mills next to them grind away. Civil War soldiers can be pictured wading across, with muskets held above their heads, hoping not to be shot, and in contrast, the Richards' children can be envisioned peacefully sitting on the river bank fishing. But most of all, what can be seen, is the natural and unchanging beauty of the river that encompassed all of those moments.

Maps

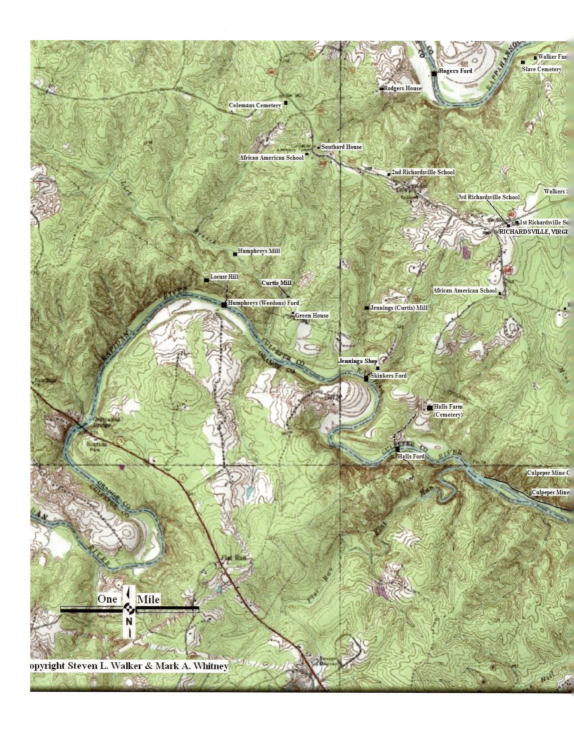

The Lower Rappahannock River Fords of Culpeper County

Steven L. Walker

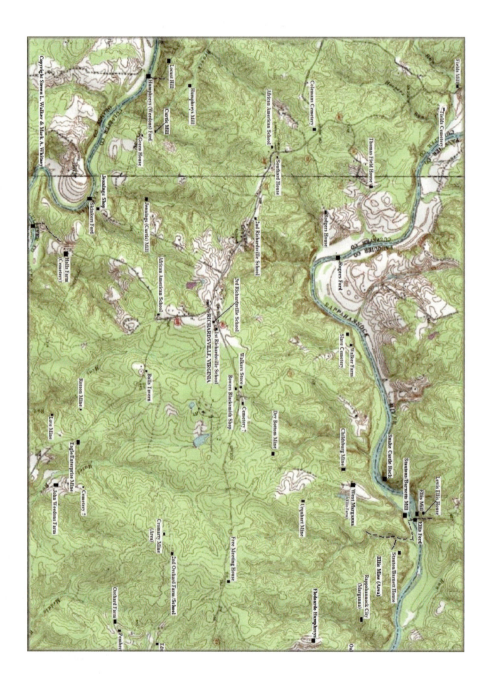

The Lower Rappahannock River Fords of Culpeper County

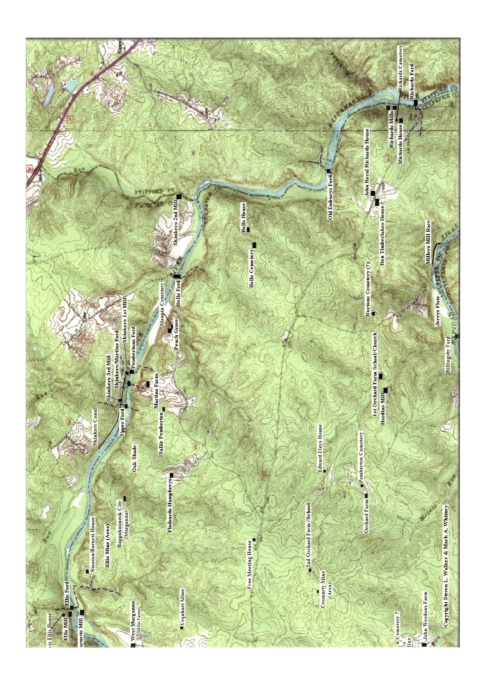

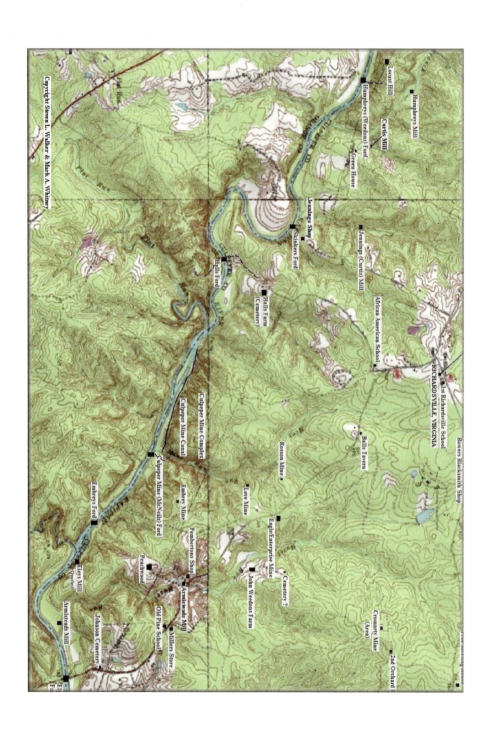

The Lower Rappahannock River Fords of Culpeper County

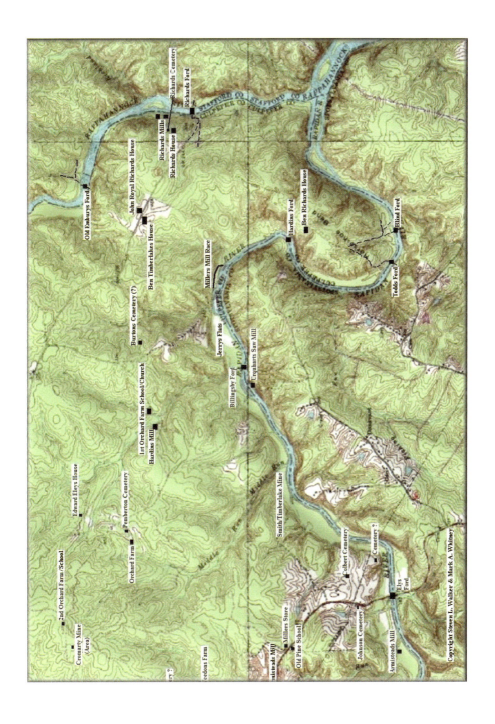

Photos

Elles Ford Tree

Ellis Ford (2006)

The Lower Rappahannock River Fords of Culpeper County

Fire Tower

Fred Ricker

Steven L. Walker

Marganna Mine Tailings

Martha Martin's Grave

Lock 16, Ellis Ford

Marganna House and Commissary

Marganna Mine

Marganna Safe

Richardsville store with Joseph Fields, 1880s. Counter is still in use

Robert Martin, Eliza Pemberton

Marganna Well

Orchard Farm School, ca. early 1900s

Richardsville store late 1800s

Richardsville store (2002)

Rock Run Bridge site

Skinkers Ford

Skinkers Ford (2008) Lock 14 - 3

Skinkers Third Mill

Appendix I

Rapidan River Fords

The locations are verified by Campbell and Dwight, *1863 Survey of Culpeper County*, Schedler; *1863 Map of Culpeper County*; Koeber, *1864 Army of the Potomac Map*; Military Atlas, *The Sketch of the Operations of the Army of the Potomac*; Garden, *1876 Map of Culpeper County*; Gilmer, *1863 Map of Culpeper County*; Paine, *1862 Map of the Rappahannock River above Fredericksburg*; Hotchkiss, *1863 Map of Fauquier County*; Hotchkiss, *1864 Maps of the Battle of Wilderness and Spotsylvania*; Scheel, *Map of Culpeper County*; Trout, *Atlas of the Rappahannock and Rapidan Rivers*, and field investigations of road traces.

1. Blind Ford: Located 1.3 miles upstream of the confluence. "*Very Bad Ford*," as stated by Lieutenant L. Norton during the Civil War. Some recent documents have mislabeled this ford as Todds Ford. The road to the ford goes past Ben Richard's house site and then forks. The left fork goes to Blind Ford. After going down the bluff, there are several approaches to the river. Near the river are mining prospects. Directly across the river is a pumping station. The location is confirmed just upstream of Hunting Run by Hotchkiss's 1864 map of the Battles of Wilderness and Spotsylvania, No.1 and No.1a.

2. Todds Ford: Located 1.7 miles above the confluence. The road to the ford is the same that passes Ben Richard's house. The right fork goes to Todds Ford. The ford was at the crest of the horseshoe bend in the river.

3. Hardins Ford: Located 2.7 miles upstream of the confluence. Some recent documents have mislabeled the name and location of the ford. Hoffman's Civil War map misspells it as Hadens Ford. Hardin had a mill nearby on Gill's Run. The location is confirmed by Hotchkiss's 1864 map of the Battles of Wilderness and Spotsylvania, No.1 and No.1a.

4. Urquharts Ford; Billingsby Ford; Jerrys Flats: Located 3.5 miles upstream of the confluence, on the Culpeper side of the river, was Jerrys Flats. In 1934, David Busnell, of the Smithsonian Institute, determined that a large Indian burial mound existed there. It was reported destroyed in a 1890's flood, scattering bones and pottery.

5. Elys Ford: Located 6.2 miles upstream of the confluence. The name is a misspelling of the local Eley family. "*Tolerably good (much used)*," as stated by Lieutenant L. Norton. It has been used throughout history, first by the Indians, then by settlers, and made famous by the Civil War. It is still a major transportation route.

6. Embreys Ford: Located just above Wilderness Run, approximately 1 mile upstream of Elys Ford. An Embrey lived nearby in Culpeper County. The ford evidently went to the Melville Mines across the river in Orange County.

7. Culpeper Mine Ford; McNeils Ford: Located 2 miles upstream of Elys Ford. "*Tolerably good*," as stated by Lieutenant L. Norton. Garden's 1876 map and Eugene

Scheel's map of Culpeper County also labels the ford as McNeils Ford. McNeil lived across the river in Orange County. The Culpeper Mining Company, chartered in 1834, built a 412-foot dam across the river upstream of the ford to divert water into a canal on the north bank. The 5,000 + foot canal powered a stamping mill to extract gold from the mines. It was a major industrial operation that had a sawmill and blacksmith shop. In 1850 the company employed 31 workers and seven miners. The Culpeper Mine was one of the most productive in the area and lasted into the early 1900s.

8. Halls Ford; McNeils Ford: Located 3.3 miles upstream of Culpeper Mine Ford. It was named after the Hall family who lived above it in Culpeper County. Schedler and Hoffman's Civil War maps also labels the ford as McNeils Ford, obviously another crossing to McNeil's house. Local lore tells of families crossing in buggies to go to Pilgrims Church.

9. Skinkers Ford: Located 4 miles upstream of Culpeper Mine Ford. S. T. Skinker lived in a house that still stands on the Orange County side of the river. David Busnell determined that it was the location of a large Indian settlement. Two fish traps can still be found in the river near the ford. Koeber's Civil War map labels it Blind Ford.

10. Humphreys Ford; Weedons Ford: Located about 1.3 miles upstream of Skinkers Ford. Captain (Colonel) Thomas Humphrey had a plantation in Culpeper County called "Locust Hill" on the bluff just upstream of the ford.

Appendix II

Mills of Chinquapin Neck

All information from Trout, *Atlas of the Rappahannock and Rapidan Rivers*; Koeber, *1864 Army of Potomac Map*; Military Atlas, *The Sketch of the Operations of the Army of the Potomac*; *Map and Profile of the Rappahannock River and its Improvement, 1848;* Schedler, *1863 Map of Culpeper County*; Paine, *1862 Map of Rappahannock River above Fredericksburg*; Couty, *Rappahannock River Canal Improvements, 1845.* Scheel's, *Map of Culpeper County*.

1. **Armistead's Mill, (Two)**: One was located on the west side of Hazel Run just south of Route 610. The other was located on the west side of Hazel Run near the Rapidan River. Which is older is not known.

2. **Staunton's Mill/Barnett's Mill**: Located at Ellis Ford in Culpeper County, it is one of the oldest mills in the area. William Staunton's house site is identified on a Lord Fairfax map of the 1740s. He sold the property to William Richard in the late 1700s. William gave it to Benjamin Barnett when he married his daughter, Isabella. Some scattered stones are all that remains. Barnett moved the mill operation across the river in the 1830s when the canal system was built. (*See Ellis Ford Chapter*)

3. **Culpeper Mine Mill**: Located on the Rapidan River as part of the Culpeper Mine operation. A 5,400 foot canal provided water to power a saw mill and a stamp mill to process gold.

4. **Curtis's Mill**: Located on a branch feeding Lick Run, below Britton Green's house site.

5. **Barnett's/Ellis's Mill**: Located on the Fauquier side of the river. The foundation still exists. (*See Ellis Ford Chapter*)

6. **Eley's/Quarles' Mill**: Located on the north side of the Rapidan River across and just upstream of where Wilderness Run enters the river.

7. **Field's Mill**: Located on Mill Run on the south side of Fields Mill Road. Remnants of the dam and the canal are still evident.

8. **Hardin's Mill**: Located on Gill's Run, just across from the first Orchard Farm Church and School.

9. **Humphrey's Mill/Curtis's Mill**: Located on Lick Run, it was built by Captain Thomas Humphreys on his Locust Hill Plantation. Later called Curtis Mill.

10. **Jennings's Mill/Curtis's Mill**: Located on the west side of Jennings Run, about a half mile before the run enters the Rapidan River. Also called Curtis Mill.

11. **Miller's Mill**: Located on the north side of the Rapidan River about three miles upstream of the confluence. The race still is evident. It may have been B. D. Miller's mill. He is shown on H. D. Garden's 1876 map of Culpeper County as living nearby with 115 acres of land.

12. **Richards's Mill**: James Richards had a grist mill and a saw mill along the Rappahannock River Canal at Richards Ford. (*See Richards Ford Chapter*)

13. **Skinker's Mill**: There were three Skinkers Mills, all located in Fauquier County. (*See Skinkers Ford Chapter*)

14. **Urquhart's Mill**: A saw mill located about four miles upstream of the confluence, on the south side of the Rapidan River. It was just upstream of where Gill's Run enters the river.

Appendix III

Gold Mines

All the information about the mines are from Eugenes Scheel's *History of Culpeper County, Scheel's Historic Site Survey of Culpeper County*, Scheel's Map of Culpeper County, various Culpeper Star Exponent articles, Civil War soldier records, Rappahannock City marketing brochure, and Fred Ricker.

Gold Mining began in "The Neck" in 1831. The area was part of a fifteen to twenty mile wide gold pyrite stretch, extending from Pennsylvania to Alabama. Some of the earliest gold mining charters were the Mill Bank Mining company of 1834, the Culpeper Mining Company of 1834 and the Eagle Mining Company of 1836. The mines operated for the next 20 years, but by the early 1860s they evidently ceased operations. The California Gold Rush and the Civil War robbed labor. Old timers report that there was a flurry of mining activity just prior to the Civil War.

A new rush of gold mining occurred in the mid 1870s and several existing mines were reincorporated and reopened. In the 1890s, another resurgence of mining activity occurred when some of the mines were purchased and reopened. With the advent of the Alaskan Gold Rush in 1897, and the exhaustion of the gold veins, mining activity waned. By 1906, the mining operations had ceased.

1. **Childsburg Mine**: The mine was located west of Ellis Ford Road, on the Lewis Ellis farm, which later became West Marganna. Before the Civil War it was considered as part of the Ellis Mines.

2. **Cromarty Mine**: Cromarty Mine was located on the east side of Route 619, in the area of the second Orchard Farm School. There were at least two shafts. Several mining pits can be found in the woods in back of the school site. Deed records show that the Urquharts owned the land in 1856 and possibly operated the mines.

3. **Culpeper Mine**: Culpeper Mine was the longest operating mine in the area. It was located on the west side of Mine Run, near the Rapidan River. The mine originated when five New York merchants bought 524 acres from Silas Wood and chartered the Culpeper Mining Company in 1834. It was also the only mining company that owned the land. They built a 412-foot dam, nine feet high, across the Rapidan River to divert water into a 5,400 foot canal. The canal was eighteen feet wide, and seven feet deep, to accommodate flatboats. The canal also provided water to power a saw mill and stamp mill.

   It was the largest mining operation in the area, consisting of three houses for laborers and miners, a blacksmith shop, a store, an ore storage building, and a powder magazine. A shaft was sunk to 120 feet, with two 35 feet side tunnels branching off. A tripod with buckets was used to raise the ore and lower the miners into the shaft. In 1850, thirty-one workers were employed, seven of them miners. Mining activity decreased after the California Gold Rush and in 1854 it had only twenty-four employees. The Civil War further robbed labor and evidently the mine closed.

In 1876, the Culpeper Gold Mine was reopened when the Virginia Gold Mining Company purchased it for $30,000. In 1882, two experienced gold miners were imported from Colorado to help work the mine. The mine continued flourishing through the 1890s, but with the Alaskan Gold Rush the mining activity decreased. As with the other mines, the operation ceased in the early 1900s. By the 1920s, only caved-in shafts and broken down machinery remained. Soon after, an attempt was made to redevelop it by the sluice gate washing method.

4. **Dry Bottom Mine**: Scheel's Historic Site Survey of Culpeper County locates the mine west of Ellis Ford Road, further from the river than the Childsburg Mines. He also states that one source says that it was never operated, but an article in the 1899 newspaper says that the mine yielded gold valued at $4 to $10 a ton. This may have been Dry Bottom Prospect, (Eagle Mines). Dry Bottom is located between the Rapidan River and the north side of Route 610, about a mile west of Elys Ford.

5. **Eagle, Enterprise, Greeley Mine; Dry Bottom Prospect**: Eagle Mine was the oldest gold mine in the area. In 1836, John W. Mitchell, Samuel Walker, and Albert G. Lucas requested a state charter for the mine. The reason for the request was that they needed capital. Mining activity decreased after the California Gold Rush and the Civil War. In 1876, it was reopened as the Enterprise Mine, with William W. Mitchell director. In the 1890s, the area was also called the Horace Greeley Mine. Some sources also call it the Dry Bottom Prospect. An 1899 newspaper article valued the ores at $4 to $10 per ton, with nuggets valued at $11 to $20. The location of the mines was on the north side of Route 610, about a mile west of Elys Ford.

6. **Ellis Mine**: Lewis Ellis, of Ellis Ford and Mill Bank, owned extensive land on the south side of the ford and operated several mines there. It was one of the county's largest. The California Gold Rush and Civil War terminated the mining operation. After Ellis's death in 1869, the mines were reopened in 1875. They were encompassed in 310 acres. There were cabins for the miners, and a blacksmith shop. In 1876, 35 employees either mined the six shafts or operated the stamp mill. Five of the shafts were at least 30 feet deep and one was more than 108 feet. After a series of accidents, and the death of a miner who fell from a bucket lowering him into a mine shaft, the mines closed. Twenty years later, in 1898, the mines briefly reopened. (*See Ellis Ford Chapter, Gold Mines*)

7. **Embrey Mine**: Scheel's map identifies the mine west of Mine Run. It is off of Embrey Ford Road, closer to the Rapidan River than Love Mine. Joseph Embrey was the chief prospector. Civil War records of Company E, 13th Virginia Infantry show that a Joseph T. Embrey was born in 1840?, was a miner, enlisted on 5/4/61at Harpers Ferry as a private, and died Sept. 1861. He could have been Joseph Embrey of Embrey Mine or his son. Embrey Mine operated up to 1903 and had a shaft more than 100 feet deep.

8. **Hall Mine**: Location unknown.

9. **Love Mine**: The mine was located on the east side of Mine Run, across the creek from Culpeper Mines. It operated from the 1850s to 1906. A 120-foot shaft was sunk in 1903.

10. **Marganna Mine:** It was originally part of the Mill Bank Mines of the 1850s. In 1891, the Powhatan Mining Company was formed when Larman Johnson purchased the land. He lived in a house located at Rappahannock City. Near his house are some very large mining shafts, one sunk to 128 feet. Attached to the house was the company's commissary and office. On the creek, down the hill from the house, was a stamping mill. In 1895, a post office was established and called Marganna, named after Johnson's two daughters, Margaret and Anna.

    Larman died sometime before 1905, and in that year the German Savings and Loan auctioned off the property to the Pittsburg Mining Company. Johnson's wife, Anna, resisted releasing the deed. She ended up moving to West Marganna, which was the Ellis farm that Larman had purchased from the Lewis Ellis's heirs. The stone foundations of the original Marganna house, commissary, and mill still exist. Next to the commissary's foundation is the company's safe. (*See Ellis Ford Chapter, Gold Mines*)

11. **Mill Bank Mines**: It was advertised in the Fredericksburg newspaper on July 1834 as being in sight of Barnett's Mill. It eventually became the Ellis and Powhatan Mines. (*See Ellis Ford Chapter, Gold Mines*)

12. **Rosson Mine**: 1836 descriptions of the mine places it on the west side of Mine Run. Rossin Mountain, actually a hill, is located on the west side of Mine Run. Later accounts place it east of Mine Run. Because of no post Civil War accounts on the mine, it may have been incorporated with the Love Mine or Culpeper Mines.

13. **Smith Tract Gold Mine, Timberlake Mine**: A hillside cut that may also be the Timberlake Gold Mine. Scheel's Historic Site Survey of Culpeper County locates it before Middle Run enters the Rapidan River.

14. **Uruqhart Mine**: Uruqhart Mine was located next to Ellis Ford Road, on the north side of Route 619. Charles, John P., and Samuel operated the mines in the 1850s. They were on the same vein of gold-bearing rock as the Ellis Mines, which were closer to the Rappahannock River and Ellis Ford.

Appendix IV

Schools; Stores; Churches; Cemeteries

All information obtained from Eugene Scheel's publications, various
Civil War maps, and Fred Ricker

Richardsville has been home to a variety of schools, stores, shops, and churches for the past two hundred years. The only store that remains is the Richardsville Country Store, and it is the heart of the village. The store deserves protection as an historic landmark, not only because of its history, but because it also represents late 19th century rural architecture. The original shelves and countertop can be seen in 19th century photographs and are still in use. The store epitomizes a time when life was simpler, and even now, remains a place where Richardsville residents gather and share their lives.

Schools:

- **African-American School, Halls Road**: Located on the right where Halls Road takes a sharp turn, one half mile from the road's entrance. It was built and operated in the early 1890s. T.O. Madden of Maddens Tavern at Lignum taught there. The school has been converted into a house and it still stands.

- **African American School**: Located on the south side of Route 610, across from the fire tower. Only the foundation remains.

- **Free Meetinghouse**: Church and school located on the corner of Ellis Mine Hunt Club Road and Route 619. Hoffman's Civil War map locates the school across the road, and other Civil War maps identify the site as ruins. Nothing of it remains.

- **Old Pine School**: Eugene Scheel's map of Culpeper County locates the school on the south side of Route 610, a quarter mile east of Hazel Run. Scheel states that when the first Orchard Farm School near Hardin's Mill ran out of enough pupils, they moved the Old Pine School to Cromarty Mine Road and renamed it "Orchard Farm School."

- **First Orchard Farm School**: The building was off of Beach Road on Gills Run. It was used as a school and a church. When there were not enough pupils, the Second Orchard Farm School was built and the remaining pupils moved there. The foundation remains.

- **Second Orchard Farm School**: Located on Cromarty Mine Road at an intersection near the Cromarty Mines. It was built in 1910 on land donated by Harold Marean. The school closed in the 1930s. The Sons of America Patriotic Club also had their meetings there. (*See photographs*)

- **First Richardsville School**: Eugene Scheels map of Culpeper County locates the school on the north side of the Methodist Cemetery.

- **Second Richardsville School**: The school was located on the north side of Route 610, two miles west of the Richardsville Country Store. A house now stands at the location. Eugene Scheel's map of Culpeper County states it was built in 1907 at a cost of $200 with funds donated by Mr. Brown of Culpeper.

- **Third Richardsville School**: Located next to the Methodist Cemetery. It burned down in the 1920s and was rebuilt. The school closed in 1936. It was used as a residence by Harry Jones until the 1940s, when it was burned from a cooking fire. The remainder of the building was dismantled and Francis Mastin sold the wood to Archie Martin for $200.

Stores:

- **Ball's/ Garthright's Tavern**: Eugene Scheel's map of Culpeper County locates the tavern about a mile east of the Richardsville Fire Department, on the north side of Route 610. It appears to be at the same location as the 1800s Weedon's farm.

- **Bailey's Tavern**: Hoffman's Civil War map identifies the store in Richardsville, on the south side of Route 610, about a half mile east of the present day Richardsville County Store. Eugene Scheel's map of Culpeper County identifies the location at the western corner of Curtis Mill Road and Route 610.

- **Beach's Store**: Built in 1934 by Eddie Embrey, who lived across the road. It was operated by Agnes Beach. Her son, Evans Beach, was captured at Corregidor, and after spending four years as a POW, died a month before the peace treaty with Japan. Beach Road is named after him. Richardsville Post Office operated out of the store in 1942. It closed in 1944 when Agnes moved to Remington.

- **Building Supply**: Located in back of Fred's Ricker's house. Built in 1910 as a building and lumber supply store. It was later used as a store by a man named Turner and then used by the Sons of the America Patriotic Club. The building eventually burned in 1968 as the result of a field fire started by a backfiring vehicle.

- **Coppage's Store**: Located directly in front of the Oakland Baptist Church. It was a combination store and house and operated by William "Bud" Coppage for a couple of years in the late 1940s. The Oakland Church bought the property and used it as rental property. In 2006, they burned it down.

- **Cole's Store**: Eugene Scheel's map of Culpeper County identifies the location at the east corner intersection of Route 610 and 619. He also labels a post office there. Presently the site is occupied by Fred Ricker's house.

- **W. D. Foster's Store**: Located on the western corner of the intersection of Route 610 and 619, in front of the present day Richardsville Country Store. Built in the 1850s, possibly by W. D.'s brother Frank Foster, who was a carpenter. After Foster, a man named Vanaukin owned and operated the store and then sold it to James B. Rogers, who operated it until 1914, when he moved to Washington. After that it was used sporadically as a store and for a long time as a post office. Frederick Taylor reopened it in 1942 and operated it as a store and post office until 1944. It stood until 1952 and was then dismantled. The lumber was used to build a house across the road.

- **Miller's Store**: Hoffman's Civil War map identifies it on the north side of Route 610, near the Eagle Mines. Jed Hotchkiss's Civil War map of Fauquier County locates the store on the eastern corner of the intersection of Route 610 and a road to Free Meetinghouse.

- **Red Front or Roger's Store**: Located on the north side of Route 610 about 300 yards west of the intersection of Route 610 and Route 619. Owned and operated by Thomas Rogers from the early 1900s to around the end of WWI. There was a shoe shop and a blacksmith shop next to it. Presently a house occupies the site. Thomas's house behind the store still stands in back of the store site.

- **Richardsville Country Store**: The store and the attached house were built in the 1880s by Joseph R. Fields. He also had a post office and was the postmaster from 1889 to 1913. After Joseph died, his wife sold the store to Bradley Hall who operated it until 1945. The store has been continually operated by various owners and is the heart of the village.

- **Smith's/ Bailey's Tavern**: Eugene Scheel's map of Culpeper County locates it at the same location as W. D. Foster's store.

- **Walker's Store**: Jed Hotchiss's Civil War map of Fauquier County locates a store at J. Walker's house on the northern side of Route 619, just before Walker Road.

Shops:

- **B S Shop**: Identified on a Schedler's Civil War map on the Rapidan River at Skinkers Ford. It most likely stands for a blacksmith shop and may be the Jenning's Shop below.

- **Bower's Blacksmith Shop**: Located on the right side of Route 619, just before the intersection with Route 703, Walker Road. It operated in the early 1900s. A concrete trough still remains.

- **Jenning's Shop**: Sketch showing the Operations or the Army of The Potomac, from Nov. 26 to Dec. 3, 1863, locates a shop near Skinkers Ford on the Rapidan River.

- **Pemberton's Shop**: Located on the south side of Route 610, on the western side of Hazel Run.

Churches:

- **Oakland Baptist Church**: Originally built in 1843, it was rebuilt in 1870. The congregation was first organized in 1843 as the Union Baptist Church. The land was donated by Zachariah Turner, with additional land donated by William Martin in 1908. The church's name came from the large oak trees on the property. Located in the rear of the church is a graveyard containing the original members. The only identifiable marker is John B. Humphrey's. His initials JBH, A 72, 1884 are scratched on it.

- **Orchard Farm Church**: Eugene Scheel states that it was a church after the pupils were moved to Old Pine School. It was located off of Beach Road, on Gills Run.

- **Publican Church**: Hoffman's Civil War map locates it at the same location as Scheel's Free Meeting House site, the western corner of Route 619 and Ellis Mine Hunt Club intersection.

- **Richardsville United Methodist Church**: Originally the site of the Free Meeting House and White's Chapel. The present church was built in 1877, no doubt because the original structure was destroyed during the Civil War. There was a Civil War Union encampment in back of the church that had numerous huts. A soldier who died of disease is said to be buried in the field beside the church. Identified as White's Chapel on Schedler's Civil War map.

Cemeteries:

Many family and slave cemeteries have been lost in time and the locations unknown. Below are the ones that are still identifiable by name, location, or both.

- **Oakland Church Cemetery**: Many of the original Richardsville residents are buried either in the cemetery in back of the church or in the cemetery across the road. Only one grave marker is still identifiable in back, John Humphreys, (JBH).

- **Bell's Cemetery**: Located across the road from Richard Bell's house site. Several graves are marked with fieldstones. Some of them are very small, indicating child mortality.

- **Burton's Cemetery**: The exact location is unknown. Eugene Scheel's map of Culpeper County locates it about a mile down Beach Road on the left (east).

- **Coleman's Cemetery**: Located on the south side of Route 610, just before the intersection of Fields Mill Road and Route 610, behind the Runyon residence.

- **Colbert's Cemetery**: Located near Elys Ford, on the north side of Route 610, now the River Hill Farm.

- **Field's Cemetery**: Located on the north side of Fields Mill Road, between Hoopers Branch and Mill Run.

- **Hall's Cemetery**: Located at the end of Halls Road on the Hall farm (*now Mastin property*). It is just east of Alexander Hall's house, which is still standing, next to Daniel Hall's house foundation. The only readable grave stone is Virginia Hall Weedon, 1840-1928. Her husband, Issaac Weedon, is also buried there.

- **Humphrey's Cemetery**: Located somewhere on the Locust Hill plantation, exact location unknown. Captain (Colonel) Thomas Humphreys is buried there.

- **Johnson's Cemetery**: Located near Elys Ford, on the south side of Route 610, now the Eagle Horse Farm.

- **Maupin's Cemetery**: Located on the Magura property at the end of Route 683. Horace Maupin, Minnie Maupin, Ella Maupin Timberlake, and a child are buried there. (*See Skinkers Ford Chapter*)

- **Pemberton's Cemetery**: Scheel's Historic Site Survey of Culpeper County locates a Pemberton cemetery near Lucy Pemberton's (Flodoardo Humphreys) house site.

- **Pemberton's Cemetery, Oak Shade**: Located near Sallie Pemberton's house site. (*See Skinkers Ford Chapter*)

- **Pemberton's Cemetery, Orchard Farm**: A large family cemetery located on the farm of Larkin Pemberton's "*Orchard Farm*." (*See Skinkers Ford Chapter*)

- **Pemberton's Slave Cemetery, Orchard Farm**: Larkin Pemberton had many slaves, so naturally there would have been a slave cemetery. The location is unknown.

- **Richards/ Barnett's Cemetery**: Located at Richards Ford, near the Richard's house site. Contains the graves of several generations of Richards and Barnetts; many of the markers identifiable. (*See Richards Ford Chapter*)

- **Richards Slave Cemetery**: Location unknown. The Richards had several slave families, including the Hawkens and Spilmans.

- **Richardsville United Methodist Church, Whites Chapel Cemetery**: Located across the road from the church. One grave, Ann Bullard Pemberton, is behind the church.

- **Slave Cemetery**: Scheel's Historic Site Survey of Culpeper County locates a slave cemetery with a question mark between Richardsville and the Rappahannock River, about a half mile north of Richardsville.

- **Walker's Slave Cemetery**: Located on the river bluff overlooking the Rappahannock River on the Walker farm, which is off of Walker Road. A fairly large cemetery, with more than a dozen graves marked with fieldstones.

- **Unknown Cemetery, Elys Ford**: Scheel's Historic Site Survey of Culpeper County locates an unknown cemetery on a bluff, a quarter mile downstream of the Elys Ford Bridge.

- **Unknown Cemetery, Walker Road**: Scheel's map of Culpeper County locates a cemetery at the northeast corner of the Walker Road and Route 619 intersection.

- **Unknown Cemetery, Weedon's property**: Located on the north side of Route 610, about a mile from Elys Ford. It is a few hundred yards north of the old Weedon house and fifty yards north of a house foundation of which the last resident was Fred Kemp. The house was vacant prior to WWII. There are four to six graves, some marked with fieldstones.

Appendix V

Company E 13th Virginia Infantry

Names in italics are believed to be from or near Richardsville; names underlined are confirmed. All information obtained from David F. Riggs, *13th Virginia Infantry*, Lynchburg, Virginia, H. E. Howard, Inc., 1988. Civil War records are sometimes incomplete or inaccurate due to the nature of the time, communication problems, or faulty recording methods. Desertions and AWOL's may in fact be POW's, sickness, detached service, transfers, or death. No further record may be KIA or MIA.

Company E was initially formed in the spring of 1861 as the "*Culpeper Riflemen*". The company was disbanded November 8, 1861 when its period of service expired. The Confederate Army was reorganized in the spring of 1862 and a new Company E was formed March 15, 1862. It went by the name "*Brandy Rifles*" and enlistments continued throughout April 1862. Very few of the original members remained in the second formation and most of the new recruits were from the Richardsville area. A militia unit from Amherst, Virginia was incorporated on April 22, 1862, but most of them soon deserted.

1. ***Allen, Thomas***: 6', light complexion, grey eyes, light hair. Enlisted in Company E at Culpeper Court House as private on 4/3/62. Absent sick May/June 1862. Wounded at Fredericksburg as part of the Battle of Chancellorsville 5/3/63. Wounded slightly at Mine Run 11/28/63. Deserted 5/13/64. Took Oath of Amnesty 3/14/65. Died 8/2/1900. *(Buried Leal Baptist Church Cemetery, Lignum VA. There was an Allen's Dam on the Rappahannock River; see Rogers Ford Chapter.)*

2. **Ashby, William Aylett**: Born 1838 in Culpeper County, 5' 8.5", light complexion, dark eyes, dark hair. Merchant. Elected sergeant in Culpeper Minute Men in 1859. Enlisted in Company B at Culpeper Court House as sergeant on 4/17/61. Promoted to Quartermaster 7/1/61. Promoted to Lieutenant in Company E on 4/22/63. Promoted to Captain 5/3/63. POW at Fisher's Hill 9/22/64; sent to Fort Delaware Prison. Took Oath of Allegiance; released 6/17/65. Married Nellie P. Alcocke; two sons. Owned a dry goods store in Baltimore, Maryland, ca. 1865 - 1870. Moved to Culpeper and a merchant for 15 years. Postmaster c. 1893. Died 1908.

3. ***Bell, George W.***: Born 1843? in Culpeper County. Enlisted in Company E at Culpeper Court House as private on 4/3/62. POW at Winchester 9/19/64. Sent to Point Lookout prison. Transferred to Aiken's Landing for exchange 3/15/65. No further record. Living in or near Fredericksburg in 1908. (*See Bells Ford Chapter*)

4. ***Bell, William F.***: Brother of George Bell. Conscripted in Company E at Caroline County as private on 3/18/1863. AWOL Sept./Oct. 1863 and three days deducted. Wounded at Lynchburg in shoulder 6/17/64. POW at Sayler's Creek 4/6/65 and

sent to Point Lookout Prison. Took Oath of Alligence and released 6/23/65. Received Cross of Honor at Fredericksburg in 1904. (*See Bells Ford Chapter*)

5. **Brooke, John L**.: Born 10/1824 in Gloucester County. Planter in Culpeper County. Enlisted in Company E at Culpeper Court House as Captain on 4/3/62. Absent sick May/June 1862 and 8/23/62. Resigned 9/2/61 due to illness. Arrested by U.S. as a "flat foot secesh" 10/23/63. Sent to Old Capital Prison and then to Point Lookout Prison. Paroled, date unknown, due to feeble condition. Incapacitated from further service. Died 2/22/69 at "Fox Neck", Culpeper County. *(Koerber's Civil War map locates a Brooke's residence and ford upstream of Germanna on the Rapidan River at Fox Neck.)*

6. *Brown, Francis J.*: Enlisted in Company E at Culpeper Court House as a private on 4/16/62. AWOL 4/26/62 thru Sept/Oct. 1863. Hospitalized in Richmond 9/16/63 thru 10/13/63; then furloughed for 35 days. No further record. *(Schedler's Civil War map locates several Brown residences near Fox Neck.)*

7. <u>**Burton, Thomas**</u>: Enlisted in Company E at Culpeper Court House as a private on 4/3/62. Present through 9/1/64. No further record. (*Eugene Scheel locates a Burton family cemetery off of Beach Road.*)

8. <u>**Burton, William P.**</u>: Enlisted in Company E at Culpeper Court House as a private on 4/3/62. Surrendered at Appomattox Court House 4/9/65. (*Eugene Scheel locates a Burton family cemetery off of Beach Road.*)

9. **Carter, Robert J.**: Enlisted in Company E at Culpeper Court House as a private on 4/18/62. Conscripted; formerly in Culpeper County militia. Discharged 6/31/62.

10. **Coffee, P. J.**: Enlisted in Company E at Culpeper Court House as private on 10/28/63. Deserted early Dec. 1863.

11. *Cole, F. M.*: Enlisted in Company E at Culpeper Court House as private on 4/12/62. AWOL Jan./Feb. 1863. Wounded probably at Somerville Ford 9/14/63. Absent sick 6/9/64 thru 9/1/64, with no record for 9/1/64 thru 12/31/64. AWOL at final muster 2/28/65. *(Scheel's map locates a Coles store at Richardsville.)*

12. *Cole, J. C.*: Enlisted in Company E at Culpeper Court House as private on 4/13/62. Absent sick 4/62 thru 6/30/62, 5/24/64 thru 6/16/64, 8/17/64. POW at Winchester 9/19/64. Sent to Point Lookout Prison and then transferred to Aiken's Island for exchange 3/15/65. *(Scheel's map locates a Coles store at Richardsville .)*

13. <u>*Coleman, Robert M.*</u>: Enlisted in Company E at Culpeper Court House as private on 4/3/62. Deserted 4/15/62. *(Scheel's map locates a Coleman cemetery near the intersection of Route 610 and Fields Mill Road; there were also Coleman*

residences near Lignum. A Robert M. Coleman is listed as one of the first 25 church members of Lignum's Leal Baptist church that was formed in 1874.)

14. Coleman, Wilson A.: Enlisted in Company E at Culpeper Court House as private on 4/3/62. AWOL 4/15/62 and declared deserter 5/1/62. *(Scheel's map locates a Coleman cemetery near the intersection of Route 610 and Fields Mill Road; there were also Coleman residences near Lignum.)*

15. <u>Curtis, Jesse</u>: Enlisted in Company E at Culpeper Court House as corporal on 4/3/62. Listed as private between 6/30/62 - 1/1/63. Detailed as carpenter 6/10/62 - ca. 3/1/63. Absent sick May/June 1863 and 7/28/63. POW Aug./Sept. 1863 thru 10/3/63. No further record. *(1870 tax records show that he owned 292 acres near Richardsville.)*

16. <u>Curtis, John F</u>.: Enlisted in Company E at Culpeper Court House as private on 4/3/62. Absent sick May/June 1862 thru 12/27/62 and May/June 1863. AWOL 4 days in Sept.?/Oct. 1863; pay deducted. AWOL 5/6/64 thru at least 9/30/64. Extra duty as a shoemaker Jan./Feb. 1865. Deserted around 4/65. POW near Richmond 4/6/65 and sent to Libby Prison through 4/10/65. No further record.

17. Curtis, Thomas O.: Born 1929?, 5' 11.25", fair complexion, blue eyes, dark brown hair. Carpenter. Enlisted in Company E at Brandy Station as sergeant on 4/17/61. Absent sick around 9/1/61 thru 11/8/61. AWOL 7/30/62 to around 3/63. AWOL one day in Sept./Oct. 1863. One days pay deducted. Wounded Spotsylvania Court House 5/19/64. POW at Fort Stedman 3/25/65. Sent to Point Lookout Prison. Took Oath of Allegiance and released 6/25/65.

18. Curtis, Walter S.: Farmer. Enlisted in Company E at Culpeper Court House as private on 4/3/62. AWOL 12/25/62 thru 1/63. AWOL four days Sept./Oct. 1863. Pay deducted. Wounded at Hactcher's Run in left leg 2/6/65, hospitalized and then furloughed 3/6/65 for 60 days. No further record. *(Gardner's 1876 map and 1870 tax records show that Walter Curtis owned 136 acres across the intersection of Jennings Road and Route 610.)*

19. Downey, William J.: Enlisted in Company E at Culpeper Court House as private on 4/3/62. Absent sick at company muster 6/30/62. No further record. *(There was a Downey family that lived across from what is now the Salvation Army Camp; 1870 tax records show a Darby Downey as owning three farms totaling 529 acres.)*

20. Ellington, John: Enlisted in Company E at Culpeper Court House as private on 4/8/62. Present through Sept./Oct. 1863. No further record. *(1870 and 1880 tax records show Virginia Ellington owning approximately 50 acres at Richardsville. She may have been John's wife or a relative; Ellingtons lived off of Beach Road; see Appendix VII, Early Residents of Richardsville.)*

21. ***Field, Daniel***: Enlisted in Company E at Culpeper Court House as Lieutenant on 4/3/62. Promoted to Captain around 9/1/62. KIA at Fredericksburg 5/3/63 while leading a charge; fell near Union cannons after being struck in the head by grape shot. *(His house site is off White Rock Road and the foundation remains.)*

22. ***Fields, James R***.: Enlisted in Company E at Culpeper Court House as private on 4/3/62. Absent sick 12/1/62 thru 3/1/63. AWOL 4/1/63 thru 7/1/63. Detached service Sept./Oct. 1863. Wounded at Bethesda Church in right leg 5/30/64; did not return to duty and declared AWOL 3/7/65. No further record. *(Owned a house on Fields Mill Road that became the Harris house.)*

23. ***Field, Thomas***: Enlisted in Company E at Culpeper Court House as corporal on 4/3/62. Absent sick 9/17/63 thru 10/26/63. POW at Winchester 9/19/64. Sent to Point Lookout Prison. Exchanged 3/15/65. No further record. *(His house on White Rock Road is still standing.)*

24. ***Grimsley, Richard T***.: Enlisted in Company E at Culpeper Court House as private on 4/12/62. Detailed as wagoner 12/21/62 thru 1/1/64. Final entry is clothing receipt dated 4/27/64. No further record. *(There are Grimsley families in Meyerstown which is near Richardsville.)*

25. **Groves, Joseph R**.: Enlisted in Company E at Culpeper Court House as private on 4/16/62. Transferred after receiving bounty from Capt. Crandall, Company I 8th LA. KIA at Cross Keys 6/8/62.

26. **Hansbrough, William L**.: 5' 7", fair complexion, gray eyes, auburn hair. Enlisted in Company E at Culpeper Court House as private on 4/3/62. Absent sick March/April thru May/June 1863. POW at Coles Hill 6/9/63. Sent Old Capital Prison; paroled 6/25/63. No record July/August 1863; present Sept/Oct. 1863. POW at Spotsylvania Court House 5/19/64 and sent to Point Lookout Prison, then Elmira Prison. Took Oath of Allegiance and released 6/19/65. *(Coles Hill is near Stevensburg and part of Hansbrough Ridge, which was part of the Battle of Brandy Station 6/9/63. The Hansbrough's home was probably within sight.)*

27. ***Heflin, John L***.: Enlisted in Company E at Somerville as private on 2/16/64. Surrendered at Appomattox Court House 4/9/65. *(John Heflin was a slave overseer of the Ellis Plantation near Richardsville. Overseer's were given exemption from the military. Later in the war his exception may have been revoked due to manpower shortages or the slaves running off. See Ellis Ford Chapter. 1870 tax records show that he owned 800 acres near Richardsville.)*

28. ***Humphreys, Lewis E***.: Enlisted at Somerville in Company E as private 8/26/63 or 12/18/63. Wounded at the Battle of Wilderness 5/6/64 and remained absent

through final muster 2/28/65. No further record. *(May be from Humphreys Plantation at Locust Hill.)*

29. Humphreys, Rufus J.: Born 1840 Farmer. Enlisted at Culpeper Court House in Company C, 7th VA Cavalry as private on 5/30/61. Discharged 6/12/62. Enlisted 4/3/62 in Company E, 13 VA Infantry as Lieutenant. Commissioned 3/15/62, but did not report to duty until 5/1/62. Present by May/June 1862. KIA at Battle of Cedar Mountain 8/9/62. *(May be from Humphrey's Plantation at Locust Hill.)*

30. Hunt, Cumberland A.: Enlisted in Company E in Orange County or at Somerville as private on 8/26/63. AWOL 6/22/64 thru 9/1/64; no record 9/64 thru 12/64. Present at final muster 2/28/65. No further record. *(There was Hunt lot in back of Fred Ricker/W.D. Foster's house in Richardsville.)*

31. <u>Jennings Edward</u>: 5 '6.25", light complexion, grey eyes, dark brown hair. Enlisted in Company E at Culpeper Court House as private on 4/3/62. Absent sick 12/21/62 to ca. 3/63. Wounded probably at Spotsylvania Court House in left foot 5/64; returned to duty 7/21/64. POW at Winchester 9/19/64 and sent to Point Lookout Prison. Took Oath of Allegiance and released 6/28/65. *(1870 tax records show Edward Jennings owned 75 acres near Richardsville.)*

32. <u>Jones, William T</u>.: Enlisted in Company E at Culpeper Court House as private on 4/3/62. Absent sick May/June 1862. Reported AWOL 9/22/62; Present Nov./Dec. 1862 thru Sept. Oct. 1863. No further record. *(There was a William S. Jones family living at the Locust Hill plantation, William T. May have been related; 1850 tax records show that four Jones families lived in the Richardsville area.)*

33. Kite, James H.: Light complexion, hazel eyes, light hair. Enlisted in Company E at New Market as private on 11/19/62. Present at final muster 2/28/65; only previous record is a clothing receipt in 12/64. POW at Petersburg 4/2/65 and sent to Point Lookout Prison. Took Oath of Allegiance and released 6/28/65.

34. Lewis, George: Enlisted in Company E at Richmond as private on 10/12/62. Present at final muster 2/28/65. No further record.

35. Luckett, Samuel R.: Born 1840?, Wheelwright. Enlisted in Company E at Brandy Station as sergeant, *Culpeper Riflemen*, on 4/17/61. Absent sick from 8/20/61 until company disbanded 11/8/61. Enlisted 4/3/62 at Culpeper Court House in Brandy Rifles as Lieutenant. KIA at Battle of Cedar Mountain 8/9/62.

36. McConchie, James H.: Enlisted in Company E at Culpeper Court House as private on 4/3/62. Absent sick without leave Nov./Dec. 1862; discharged 1/10/63 for being under aged. POW at Brandy Station 8/1/63; sent to Old Capital Prison and then to Point Lookout Prison. Exchanged 2/10/65; hospitalized in Richmond

2/16/65. No further record. *(1870 tax records show John W. McConchie owned 20 acres at Richardsville; may be related.)*

37. **McMurran, Joseph**: Enlisted in Company E at Culpeper Court House as private on 4/3/62. Absent sick 8/11/62 thru 9/2/62. Wounded in the left leg at the Battle of Fredericksburg by shell 12/13/62; returned to duty ca. 1/63. Wounded at 2nd Battle of Fredericksburg 5/3/63. Present at final muster 2/28/65. Paroled at Richmond 4/26/65.

38. **Martin, John S.**(or J.): Enlisted in Company E at Culpeper Court House as private on 4/3/62. Promoted to corporal ca. 7/62 - 12/62. Promoted to sergeant ca. 1/63 - 9/64. POW at Winchester 9/19/64. No further record.

39. **Newcomer, Emanuel**: Enlisted in Company E at Culpeper Court House as private on 4/19/62. Formerly in the Culpeper militia. Wounded at Gaines Mill 6/27/62. Sent home to recuperate and deserted.

40. *<u>Pemberton, Thomas L</u>*.: Dark complexion, grey eyes, black hair. Enlisted in Company E at Culpeper Court House as private on 4/3/62. Absent sick 7/1/64 thru 9/1/64. No record 10/64 thru 12/64 except for clothing receipt dated 12/24/64. POW at High Bridge 4/6/65 and sent to Point Lookout Prison. Took Oath of Allegiance and released 6/16/65. *(See Skinkers Ford Chapter)*

41. *<u>Pemberton, William P</u>.*: Enlisted in Company E at Culpeper Court House as sergeant on 4/3/62. Wounded at Gaines Mill 6/27/62. Recommended for promotion to 2nd Lt. after Battle of Cedar Mountain ca. 8/62. Apparently wounded at Fredericksburg in left thigh 12/13/62, contusion by shell. Absent sick 12/15/62 thru 12/31/62. Cited for distinguished service at Fredericksburg 5/3/63 - 5/4/63. Absent sick 10/11/63 ca. 12/2/63. Present 9/1/64. No further record. *(Family history tells that he was killed in battle, probably at Winchester 9/19/64. See Chapter on Skinkers Ford.)*

42. **Powell, Hugh Ptolemy**: Born 1840. Student. Enlisted at Harpers Ferry in Company A as private. Absent sick 6/61 and Sept./Oct. 1861. Promoted to sergeant 4/23/62. Back to private 5/15/62 and then to corporal ca. Sept./Oct. 1863. Demoted back to private by March/April 1864. Promoted to Lt. 1/10/65. Transferred to Company E 8/1/64. Unofficial source says that he was KIA on 3/25/65 at the Battle of Fort Stedman.

43. *Redd, Phillip D.*: Enlisted in Company E at Culpeper Court House as sergeant on 4/3/62. MWIA at Fredericksburg in leg 12/13/62, leg amputated. Died 1/12/63 at General Hospital No. 12 in Richmond. *(Civil War maps locate a Redd residence on Mountain Run, just upstream of Stone's-Paoli Mill.)*

44. *<u>Rodgers, John F</u>.*: Enlisted in Company E at Culpeper Court House as private on 4/3/62. Detailed as wagoner 7/15/62 thru 6/30/63. Sick 10/62; no record July/

August 1863. Detailed as wagoner 12/63 and 6/5/64 thru 9/1/64.; no record 9/64 thru 10/64. Extra duty as shoemaker Jan./Feb. 1865. POW 4/6/65; sent to Libby Prison 4/7/65. No further record. *(May be related to the Rodgers' of Rodger's Ford, or his name is a misspelling of James F. Rodgers of Rodger's Ford.)*

45. **Sisson, William T.**: Enlisted in Company E at Standardsville as sergeant on 4/29/62. Sisson originally volunteered in another company but was mustered into Company E. Present at company muster 6/30/62. No further official record. Unofficial source says he was wounded at the Battle of Cedar Mountain 8/9/62. Died 1862.

46. **Smith, D. R.**: Enlisted at New Market in Company E as private on 1/8/64. AWOL from 12/8/64 through final muster 2/28/65. No further record.

47. **Smith, John R.**: Listed in Company E as a private. The only records are a clothing receipt on 11/18/64. Paroled at Charlottesville 5/18/65.

48. *<u>Smith, Johnson</u>*: Enlisted in Company E at Culpeper Court House as private on 4/3/62. Detailed as wagoner 6/10/62 thru 10/9/63; then apparently hospitalized until 8/6/64 and furloughed. Final muster 2/28/65 lists him as a deserter. *(Postmaster of Richardsville 1858; Richardsville originally was called Smith's Tavern.)*

49. *<u>Smith, Martin Vanburen</u>*: Born 5/16/46 in Culpeper County. Enlisted in Company E at Culpeper Court House as private on 4/3/62. Detailed as a wagoner 6/10/62; returned to regiment by 1/63, possibly earlier. Absent sick 6/9/63 thru 6/30/63; no record July/August 1863. Present at final muster 2/28/65. No further record. Married Mollie J. in 1869. Farmer in Spotsylvania County. Died at Richardsville 6/22/31. Buried at Oakland Baptist Church, Richardsville. *(Richardsville originally was called Smith's Tavern.)*

50. **Strother, Philip**: Born in Culpeper County. Educated at Columbia College (George Washington University), married Nannie Pendleton, and had 7 children. Served one year as private, then discharged due to myopia. Appointed Provost Marshal from civilian status 11/19/62. Promoted to Lt. of Company E on 12/13/62. Wounded at Spotsylvania Court House in left lung 5/12/64 and retired to invalid Corps 12/12/65. Lawyer. Died before 1929.

51. *Suthard, John F.*: Enlisted in Company E at Culpeper Court House as private on 4/3/62. Absent sick May/June 1862; no record 7/62 thru 10/62. "Sent to Lynchburg Hospital" Nov./Dec. 1862. Died 1/13/63, General Hospital No. 2, Lynchburg, pneumonia, buried Lynchburg City Cemetery. *(Southard was pronounced as Suthard in Richardsville. The Southards of Southard's crossing were most likely Suthards.)*

52. *Suthard, William T.*: Enlisted in Company E at Culpeper Court House as private on 4/3/62. Hospitalized 5/62. Died of enteritis 5/27/62 at General Hospital No. 1, Lynchburg. *(Southard was pronounced as Suthard in Richardsville. The Southards of Southard's crossing were most likely Suthards.)*

53. *<u>Tyson, Joseph</u>*: Enlisted in Company E at Culpeper Court House as private on 4/3/62. AWOL 5/10/62 thru Jan./Feb. 1863. Deserted 5/3/63. POW 9/25/63. No further record. *(1880 tax records show that Joseph Tyson owned 11 acres at Richardsville.)*

54. *Walker, Alexander D.*: Enlisted in Company E at Culpeper Court House as sergeant on 4/3/62. Hospitalized 8/15/62 thru ca.1/63. Wounded at Fredericksburg 5/3/63. Wounded in left leg at Winchester 9/19/64. No further record. *(There was a large Walker Farm near Richardsville that was on the Rappahannock River.)*

55. *Walker, John S.*: Enlisted in Company E at Culpeper Court House as private on 4/3/62. Absent sick 5/1/62 thru Jan./Feb. 1863. Absent sick 8/19/63 thru Sept./Oct. 1863; no record 11/63 thru 4/64. Wounded at Spotsylvania Court House 5/12/64 and absent recuperating through 9/1/64. No further record. *(There was a large Walker Farm near Richardsville on the Rappahannock River.)*

56. *Wharton, Staunton*: Born 1825?, 5' 11.25", fair complexion, blue eyes, brown hair. Farmer. Enlisted in the Culpeper Riflemen at Brandy Station as private on 4/17/61. Absent sick when company disbanded 11/8/61. Enlisted in Company E at Culpeper Court House as private on 4/3/62. AWOL May/June 1862. Wounded in the head at Chantilly 9/1/62. Absent sick 6/9/63 thru Sept./Oct. 1863; no record 11/63 thru 4/64. POW at Petersburg 4/2/65 and sent to Point Lookout Prison. Took Oath of Allegiance and released 6/22/65. *(An 1876 map shows a Wharton house on Mountain Run upstream of where it enters the Rappahannock River; Scheel's map also shows a Whorton cemetery there.)*

57. **Woodville, Robert E.**: Enlisted in Company E at Culpeper Court House as private on 4/3/62. Died 3/1/63 in camp near Port Royal.

Amherst County Militia

1. **Allen, James Henry**: Enlisted in Company E at Gordonsville as private on 4/22/62. *Conscripted from the Amherst County militia.* AWOL 11/29/62 to May/June 1863. Court-martialed 1863 and forfeited 4 months pay. Deserted 12/6/64.

2. **Allen, R. H.**: Enlisted in Company E at Gordonsville as private on 4/22/62. *Conscripted from the Amherst County militia.* Absent sick 12/4/62 thru 7/1/63; no further record July/August 1863. Mortally wounded in action at Winchester, head wound, 9/19/64. Died 1864.

3. **Allen, William P.**: Enlisted in Company E at Gordonsville as private on 4/22/62. *Conscripted from the Amherst County militia.* Absent sick 1/23/63 and returned either voluntarily or by arrest. Wounded at the Battle of Wilderness 5/6/64 and remained absent recuperating through final muster 2/28/65. No further record.

4. **Angus, William**: Enlisted in Company E at Gordonsville as private on 4/22/62. *Conscripted from the Amherst County militia.* AWOL 6/1/62 thru 4/1/63. POW at Spotsylvania Court House 5/19/64; sent to Point Lookout Prison. Died 8/2/64 at Point Lookout.

5. **Bowls, W.**: Enlisted in Company E as private at Gordonsville on 4/22/62. *Conscripted from the Amherst County militia.* Deserted 6/1/62.

6. **Brown, Field T.**: Enlisted in Company E at Gordonsville as private on 4/22/62. *Conscripted from the Amherst County militia.* Sent to hospital after enlistment and deserted 4/26/62.

7. **Burford, S. M.**: Enlisted as a private in Company E at Gordonsville on 4/22/62. *Conscripted from the Amherst County militia.* Deserted 6/1/62.

8. **Byass, Henry**: Enlisted as a private in Company E at Gordonsville on 4/22/62. *Conscripted from the Amherst County militia.* Discharged 6/23/62.

9. **Cash, Ludwell**: Born ca. 1823-1828. Enlisted as a private in Company E at Gordonsville on 4/22/62. *Conscripted from the Amherst County militia.* AWOL 6/13/62. Arrested ca. Jan./Feb. 1863. Discharged 4/18/63 on Writ of Habeas corpus at Bowling Green.

10. **Coffey, Charles E.**: Enlisted as a private in Company E at Gordonsville on 4/22/62. *Conscripted from the Amherst County militia.* Deserted 6/1/62.

11. **Coffey, Henry**: Enlisted as a private in Company E at Gordonsville on 4/22/62. *Conscripted from the Amherst County militia.* Deserted 6/1/62. Returned sometime after 7/1/63. Deserted 6/17/64.

12. **Coffey, James**: Born 8/23/36. Enlisted as a private in Company E at Gordonsville on 4/22/62. *Conscripted from the Amherst County militia.* Deserted 8/12/62. Returned sometime after 7/1/63. Court-martialed 3/7/64. Deserted 6/17/64. Died 12/30/15. Buried in the Coffey family cemetery, Amherst VA.

13. **Coffey, John**: Born 5/8/36. Enlisted as a private in Company E at Gordonsville 4/22/62. *Conscripted from the Amherst County militia.* Deserted 6/1/62. Died 12/1/07. Buried in the Coffey family cemetery, Amherst VA.

14. **Coffey, William**: Born 11/10/43. Enlisted as a private in Company E at Gordonsville 4/22/62. *Conscripted from the Amherst County militia.* Deserted 6/1/62. Farmer at Alto, Amherst County. Died 6/13/27. Buried in the Coffey family cemetery, Amherst VA.

15. **Coleman, Rufus**: Born 1821? Enlisted as a private in Company E at Gordonsville 4/22/62. Deserted 4/26/62. Discharged on Writ of Habeas Corpus 4/18/63.

16. **Crawford, James M.**: Enlisted as a private in Company E at Gordonsville on 4/22/62. *Conscripted from the Amherst County militia*. Absent sick May/June 1862. Deserted 6/1/62. Arrested 10/27/63. Court-martialed 3/17/64. Wounded at Spotsylvania Court House in left hand 5/64 before 5/16/64 when he was hospitalized and remained absent through final muster 2/28/65 due to wound. No further record.

17. **Crawford, William E.**: Enlisted as a private in Company E at Gordonsville on 4/22/62. *Conscripted from the Amherst County militia.* Deserted 6/1/62.

18. **Cundriff, Isaac**: Enlisted as a private in Company E at Gordonsville on 4/22/62. *Conscripted from the Amherst County militia.* Deserted 6/1/62.

19. **Harrison, Lewis**: Born 1823-1828. Enlisted as a private in Company E at Gordonsville on 4/22/62. *Conscripted from the Amherst County militia.* AWOL 6/1/62 thru 4/9/62. Transferred to 58th VA Infantry 4/9/63. Another record says he was discharged from the 13th VA 4/18/63 on Writ of Habeas Corpus.

20. **Hicks, Moses**: Enlisted as a private in Company E at Gordonsville on 4/22/62. *Conscripted from the Amherst County militia.* Deserted 6/15/62. Returned 9/64. Ordered for guard duty by medical examining board 9/12/64.

21. **Hudson, Shannon**: Enlisted as a private in Company E at Gordonsville on 4/22/62. *Conscripted from the Amherst County militia.* AWOL 6/15/62 until transferred to 49th VA Infantry 4/9/63.

22. **Hudson, Shelton**: Born 1822? Enlisted as a private in Company E at Gordonsville on 4/22/62. *Conscripted from the Amherst County militia.* AWOL 6/15/62 until arrested Jan/Feb. 1863. Transferred to 49th VA Infantry 4/9/63.

23. **Knight, Richard H.**: Enlisted as a private in Company E at Gordonsville on 4/22/62. *Conscripted from the Amherst County militia.* Absent sick from 4/62 until 5/15/62 when he deserted.

24. **Lockheart, William A.**: Enlisted as a private in Company E at Gordonsville on 4/22/62. *Conscripted from the Amherst County militia.* Sick 10/11/63 - 4/64. MWIA in head, battle and date not reported. POW in Petersburg hospital 4/3/65.

Died 4/11/65 or 5/0/65 at Fair Ground Post Hospital, Petersburg. Buried in hospital cemetery.

25. **McConchie, Robert A.**: 5' 9.75", dark complexion, blue eyes, brown hair. Enlisted as a private in Company E at Culpeper Court House on 4/22/62. *Conscripted from the Amherst County militia.* Wounded at Fredericksburg 5/3/63. AWOL 1/65. Present at final muster 2/28/65; POW at Petersburg 4/2/65. Sent to Point Lookout Prison. Took Oath of Allegiance and released 6/15/65.

26. **McDaniel, Lindsey**: Born 1819? Enlisted as a private in Company E at Gordonsville on 4/22/62. *Conscripted from the Amherst County militia.* AWOL 6/16/62 - Nov./Dec. 1862. Present and under arrest Jan./Feb.1863. Discharged 4/18/63 on Writ of Habeas Corpus.

27. **Miller, Sheffey**: Born 1819? Enlisted as a private in Company E at Gordonsville on 4/22/62. *Conscripted from the Amherst County militia.* Hospitalized 5/27/62. AWOL from 6/15/62 until Jan./Feb. 1863 when he was present under arrest; remained in this capacity until discharged 4/18/63 on Writ of Habeas Corpus.

28. **Noel, Mansfield**: Enlisted as a private in Company E at Gordonsville on 4/22/62. *Conscripted from the Amherst County militia.* Deserted 5/23/62.

29. **Peters, Charles C.**: Enlisted as a private in Company E at Gordonsville on 4/22/62. *Conscripted from the Amherst County militia.* Deserted 6/23/62. Died by 1902.

30. **Pool (Poole), Henry**: Enlisted as a private in Company E at Gordonsville on 4/22/62. *Conscripted from the Amherst County militia.* AWOL from 8/23/62 until arrested March/April 1863. Court-martialed May/June 1863 and 8 months pay deducted. Hospitalized 7/18/63. Absent sick from 8/30/63 until death 11/1/63 at General Receiving Hospital at Gordonsville of pneumonia.

31. **Sandige, V. F.**; Enlisted as a private in Company E at Gordonsville on 4/22/62. *Conscripted from the Amherst County militia.* Deserted 6/15/62.

32. **Staples, J.**: Enlisted as a private in Company E at Gordonsville on 4/22/62. *Conscripted from the Amherst County militia.* Deserted 5/10/62.

33. **Staten, Benjamin A.**: Enlisted as a private in Company E at Gordonsville on 4/22/62. *Conscripted from the Amherst County militia.* Deserted 5/15/62 and arrested 10/27/63; court-martialed 1/27/64. Died 2/27/64 at General Hospital No. 13 Richmond, typhoid fever.

34. **Tinsley, James**: Enlisted as a private in Company E at Gordonsville on 4/22/62. *Conscripted from the Amherst County militia.* Deserted 5/15/62.

35. **Tomlin, Thomas**: Enlisted as a private in Company E at Gordonsville on 4/22/62. *Conscripted from the Amherst County militia.* Deserted 5/10/62.

36. **Ware, John J.**: Enlisted as a private in Company E at Gordonsville on 4/22/62. *Conscripted from the Amherst County militia.* AWOL 5/15/62-12/62. Under arrest, Jan./Feb. 1863. Discharged, Writ of Habeas Corpus 5/1/63.

37. **Wheeler, Henry**: Enlisted as a private in Company E at Gordonsville on 4/22/62. *Conscripted from the Amherst County militia.* Deserted 5/20/62. Listed as "under arrest" sent to Richmond 5/64-9/64, with Co. A Ward's Battalion C. S. Prisoners and released from prison at Lynchburg 7/64. Filed pension application 1902.

38. **White, Arthur**: Born 8/31/24, married Mary E. Sandidge and had five children. Enlisted as a private in Company E at Gordonsville on 4/22/62. *Conscripted from the of Amherst County militia.* Deserted 5/20/62, discharged 5/1/63 on Writ of Habeas Corpus. Unofficial source says he later served in the 2nd Va. Cavalry. Living in Lexington in 1884.

39. **Wood, Richard H.**: Enlisted as a private in Company E at Gordonsville on 4/22/62. *Conscripted from the Amherst County militia.* Deserted 6/1/62, died 7/31/98, spinal meningitis.

Appendix VI

Ambushes and Engagements
Chinquapin Neck Fords
Sept. - April 63/64

After the Gettysburg campaign, the armies settled in on the Rappahannock River, Lee on the south side and the Union army on the north. In late August, Lee moved to the south side of the Rapidan River, but his cavalry stayed in Culpeper County, where they continued to patrol the fords. During this time, the Union 3rd Infantry Brigade of the 2nd Division, 12th Corps was stationed across the Rappahannock River fords of Chinquapin Neck. Custer's Cavalry Brigade, including the 1st Vermont and 1st Michigan, was assigned to picket the fords. The Union Army remained there until late September. Even though Lee had retreated to the Rapidan River, guerilla activity continued until the Mine Run Campaign.

Skinkers Ford; *Sept 1, 1863*, O.R. 29, pt. 2, pp. 151-152.
- Brigadier General Geary reported, "... *rebels, to the number of 10 to 15 crossed on the dam, attacked the pickets and after **killing one** and scattered the rest as they recrossed.*"
- Custer's Brigade, including the 1st Vermont and 1st Michigan Cavalry, had picket duty on the north side of the Rappahannock River.
- The 149th NY was also stationed across the river.
- This had to be Confederate guerillas or cavalry because Lee's Army was on the other side of the Rapidan River at Orange.

Richards Ford; *Sept. 26, 1863*, O.R. 29, pt. 1, p. 198.
- 1st Vermont Cavalry stationed on the north side of the river was ambushed.
- One Lt. and 13 men captured, *1 man killed*.
- Lt. Col. Preston reported Confederate guerilla bands spotted, one party of 30 and another party of

In late November, General Meade decided to attack Lee before winter set in and the soldiers built winter camps. He believed the Confederate army was at half strength because Longstreet's Corps was in Tennessee. Meade's plan was to cross the Rapidan River at Jacobs, Germanna and Culpeper Mine Fords and attack Lee's right flank near Mine Run. In the process, the 1st and 5th Corps went through Richardsville and crossed at the Culpeper Mine Ford. Kilpatrick's Cavalry Division was ordered to picket the Rapidan Fords. The Reserve Cavalry Brigade guarded Richardsville.

Because of tardy Union troop movements, Lee was prepared for the attack, and Meade decided to retreat back across the Rapidan. During Dec. 1 and 2, Meade's army crossed back over the Rapidan River. The 2nd and 3rd Corps used the Culpeper Mine Ford on the retreat. Two brigades of the 3rd Corps and Greggs Cavalry Division were ordered to remain at Richardsville as rear guard while the rest of the army marched back to their camps.

Elys Ford; *Nov. 26, 1863*, Jaynes, *The Killing Ground*, Alexandria, VA, Time-Life Books, 1986, pp. 8-29
- Union and Confederate cavalry clashed, thus beginning the Mine Run Campaign.
- At that time Meade's forces numbered 89,000 and Lee's 48,000.

Culpeper Mine Ford; *Nov, 25, 1863*. O. R. 29, pt. 1, pp. 1004 - 1008; O.R. 29, pt. 2, pp. 480, 229

- Union forces arrived round 10.00 am.. No opposition to the crossing. Two Confederate vedettes were captured. By 12:15 p.m., two pontoon bridges were in place.
- Three additional roads to the ford were constructed, one of them corduroyed. An additional road was added on the other side.
- Wagons were ordered to remain at Richardsville throughout the campaign. Only ambulances and half of the ammunition wagons were allowed to cross the Rapidan.

Elys Ford near Jennings Farm; *Dec. 1, 1863*, O.R. 29, pt. 1, p. 6.

- Skirmish at Jennings Farm. No circumstantial report on file in Official Records
- There was a ford on the Rapidan River at the Jennings farm. It was called Skinkers Ford (*not to be confused with the Rappahannock River's Skinkers Ford*). Evidently, some troops used the crossing during the retreat or the Confederates crossed to probe the retreat.

Elys Ford, *Dec. 2, 1863*, O.R. 29, pt. 1, p. 809; O.R. 29, pt. 2, p. 538.

- Gregg's cavalry crossed back into Culpeper County via Elys Ford. His 1st Maine Cavalry picketed the road from Elys Ford to Richardsville through Dec. 4.
- Gregg reported on Dec. 3 that, "*Some of the enemy's cavalry were seen opposite Ellis Ford yesterday. I suppose these were guerrilla scouts.*"

Ellis Ford; *Dec. 3, 1863*, O.R. 29, pt. 1, p. 6.

- Skirmish at Ellis Ford. No circumstantial report on file in Official Records.

In early December, after the Mine Run Campaign and crossing back into Culpeper County, the Union army went into winter camps. Their main supply station was at Brandy Station. Lee went into winter camps across the Rapidan River in Orange County. His supply station was at Orange. The armies stayed in their camps until early May 1864 and the Battle of the Wilderness.

During the winter, to protect the Union army from surprise attacks and guerilla ambushes, cavalry was assigned to guard the Rappahannock and Rapidan Rivers fords. Because of the many fords in the area, a full cavalry brigade was assigned to Richardsville. It was the 1st Brigade, of the 3rd Cavalry Division. The commander was General Henry Davies. The brigade consisted of the 2nd NY, 5th NY, and 18 PA Cavalry regiments.

The 1st Brigade's base camp was in back of the Richardsville Methodist Church. Small stone piles are what is left of their hut sites. The brigade's reserve camp was at Southard's Crossing, (present fire tower). Koeber's Civil War map shows that 44 troopers were kept at the base camp and 100 were kept at the reserve camp. On March 17, the 18th PA was assigned across the river at Grove Church. From Richardsville, squads of troopers took turns guarding the major intersections and river crossings. The intersections generally had nine men assigned to them, while the fords had six. Mounted troopers patrolled the roads every thirty minutes. The duty was hazardous and throughout the winter the brigade was subjected to attacks.

Ellis Ford; *Jan. 12, 1864*, O.R. 33, pt. 1, p. 1.

- Affair near Ellis Ford. No circumstantial report on file in Official Records.

Elys Ford; *Jan.13, 1864*, O.R. 33, pt. 1, p. 19.

- A party of dismounted rebels crossed the Rapidan River on the ice and ambushed the 18th PA Cavalry on the road to Elys Ford (Route 610).
- One non-commissioned officer and six men captured.

Elys Ford; *Jan. 17, 1864*, O.R. 33, pt. 1, p. 20.

- One sergeant and eight men returning from Ely's Ford to Richardsville were fired upon from both sides and rear by dismounted men in dense pine woods.
- One man killed, *two wounded*, two captured.

Ellis Ford; *Jan 17, 1864*, O.R. 33, pt. 1, pp. 20, 392

- One Sergeant and seven men captured returning from Ellis Ford to Richardsville
- Custer reported one Captain and seven men captured.

Ellis Ford; *Jan. 22, 1864*, O.R. 33, pt. 1, pp. 20, 402.

- Davies reported that Lt. Munson, of the 5th NY Cavalry, left Southards Crossing (fire tower) with 30 men at 2:30 p.m. Within a short distance from the ford, in dense pine woods, they were fired upon by 60 - 70 dismounted men, **most of them wearing U.S. Blue overcoats**.
- One man killed, *six wounded*, four captured, three horses killed.

On February 6, 1864, Kilpatrick crossed the Rapidan River at Culpeper Mine Ford with a force of 1,360 men to make a reconnaissance in force. It was either to determine Lee's position on the Rapidan River or a diversionary action for an infantry demonstration occurring upstream at Mortons Ford. At the same time, another cavalry division made a reconnaissance at Barnetts Ford, above Mortons Ford. During the cavalry diversions, three Union brigades of the 2nd Infantry Corps crossed the Rapidan River at Mortons Ford, captured the enemy's picket, and then were repulsed. It all seems to be a reconnaissance in force to determine the enemy's position and strength.

Culpeper Mine Ford; February 6-7, 1864, O.R. 33, p. 114, pp. 140 - 141, 526, 622.

- Scattered the Confederate picket of six men while crossing the ford.
- Kilpatrick wrote, *"the ford very bad, impossible for artillery or wagons to cross."*
- Davies states on February 6, *"The command marched across Culpeper Ford, on the Rapidan, to Culpeper Mine, capturing 10 enemy's pickets."*
- Kilpatrick was ordered to return back across the Rapidan River on February 7.

The 1st Brigade remained at Richardsville throughout the winter except from February 28 thru March 14. During that period they were part of the Kilpatrick/Dahlgren raid on Richmond to liberate prisoners. Kilpatrick's raid involved 3,550 troopers and began at Elys Ford. During Davies's absence, 84 troopers from the 1st Maine, 2nd Brigade, 2nd Division were assigned to the Elys Ford area.

Elys Ford; February 28, 1864, O.R. 33, pp. 169, 181, 183, 189, 203, 780; Louis N. Beaudry, *Records of the 5th NY Cavalry*, Albany, 1874.

- With the aid of scouts, Lieutenant Merritt and a party of 15 men of the 5th NY crossed and captured the Confederate picket consisting of a Captain, Lieutenant, and 14 men. They were in a house some distance back from the river.

- The Captain was the officer of the day who stopped for the night on his tour of inspection.
- The Lieutenant and 14 men belonged to a NC cavalry regiment. The Confederate's report stated that, "*. . . a small body was piloted over the river by a citizen.*"
- Kilpatrick's signal officer reported that they left Stevensburg at 7:00 p.m. and arrived at Elys Ford about 11:00 p.m. Dalgren and a detachment of 600 proceeded them by about an hour. He stated that the night was beautiful and "*... the moon threw a silvery light upon the Rapidan waters when we forded it.*"

Elys Ford; *March 4 thru April, 1864,* O.R. 33, p. 640, 891.

While Kilpatrick was away on the Richmond raid, Custer sent a reconnaissance to Elys Ford. They scattered a small Confederate cavalry picket. One hundred and fifty men crossed over and scoured the countryside, finding no enemy.

In April, the 1st Connecticut Cavalry was transferred to the 1st Brigade and they arrived with several problems. First, they were issued Smith carbines which they considered unreliable; one officer called them "*worthless*." Second, they had 85 men that had deserted from the enemy's cavalry, took the Oath of Allegiance, and been assigned to their unit. The commander felt they could not be relied on in action because if they were captured, they would be summarily punished. He kept them in camp, anxiously wanting them to be transferred to the rear. The Connecticut regiment also was suffering from the weather because they had no winter quarters built and only had shelter halves for protection.

The 1st brigade's leadership changed in April. Grant was placed in charge of the Union Armies, and in turn, reorganized the Army of the Potomac. He eliminated the 1st and 3rd Infantry Corps and placed Sheridan in charge of the Cavalry Corps. Kilpatrick was transferred to the western theater and Wilson assumed command of the 3rd Cavalry Division. Davies was transferred to the 2nd Cavalry Division and Colonel Bryan made commander of the 1st Brigade.

Ellis Ford; *April 17, 1864*, O.R. p. 1034.

- During April, units of the 2nd Cavalry Division patrolled Ellis Ford on the north side of the river.
- On April 17, the 10th NY Cavalry had **one man killed, (Henry Jordon),** and *three badly wounded* near Ellis Ford.
- On April 21, 1864, **one of the wounded died, (S. D. Lawrence),** from his wounds on April 17.

Richardsville Methodist Church, *Winter; 1864,* **Fred Ricker**

- During the winter, one trooper died of disease while in camp in back of the church. He was buried in the field on the east side of the church.

Casualties, *Sept. 1863 thru April 1864*:
(*Does not include casualties from the Mine Run Campaign or the Kilpatrick Dahlgren Raid. There are undoubtedly unrecorded casualties.*)

Killed: 6
Died of disease: 1
Wounded: 10
Captured: 35
Total: 52

The organization of the 1st Brigade from October 1863 thru May 1864:

Oct. 10, 1863, O.R. 29, pt.1, p. 224
Brig. General Henry E. Davies, Jr.
2nd NY, Lieut. Col. Otto Harhaus
5th NY, Major John Hammond
18th PA, Major Harvey B. Van Vorhis
1st West VA, Major Charles E. Capeheart

Nov. 20, 1863; O.R. 29, pt. 2, p. 676
Brig. General Henry E. Davies, Jr.
2nd NY, Lieut. Col. Otto Harhaus
5th NY, Major John Hammon
18th PA, Col. Timothy M. Bryan, Jr.
1st West VA, Major Harvey Farabee

Dec. 31, 1863; O.R. 29, pt. 2, p. 606
Brig. General Henry E. Davies, Jr.
2nd NY, Lieut. Col. Otto Harhaus
5th NY, Major Amos H. White
18th PA, Col. Timothy M. Bryan, Jr.

April 30, 1864; O.R. 33, p. 1044
Col. Timothy M. Bryan Jr.
2nd NY, Lieut. Col. Otto Harhaus
5th NY, Major Amos H. White
18th PA, Lieut. Col. William P. Brinton
1st Conn., Major Erastus Blakeslee

The brigade armament: 2nd NY, Sharps, Spencer and Burnside carbines; 5th NY, Sharps rifles, Spencer, Merrill carbines, and Spencer rifles; 18th PA, Merrill carbines, Earl J. Coates and Dean S. Thomas, *An Introduction to CIVIL WAR SMALL ARMS*, Gettysburg, PA, Thomas Publications. 1990, pp. 93-94.

Appendix VII

Early residents of the Richardsville area

All information was obtained from Culpeper County Will Books, Deed Records, Koplend Geneology, Tax Records, 13th VA Regimental History, Eugene Scheel's publications, Civil War maps, National Archives, and Fred Ricker. Not all inclusive of the area's early residents.

- **Allison, Robert**: Richardsville's Justice of the Peace in the early 1900s. Lived near the end of Jennings Road, on the right.

- **Allison, T. L.**: Lived near the end of Jennings Road. 1880 tax records show that he owned 300 acres, 100 of them improved, valued at $3,000, 5 horses, 5 milk cows, 13 cattle, 2 work oxen, 13 cattle, and 20 swine.

- **Bailey, Charles C.**: Postmaster of Smiths Tavern (Richardsville)10/12/1835 and 1/20/1846.

- **Barnett, Benjamin N. Sr.**: Married Isabella Richards, daughter of William Richards. His home and mill were located at Ellis/ Barnetts Ford, which was obtained from William when he married his daughter. (*See Ellis Ford Chapter, Mills*)

- **Barnett, Benjamin F.**: Son of Benjamin Sr. 1850 tax records show that he owned 300 acres, 175 of them improved, valued at $2,000, 5 horses, 4 milk cows, 4 work oxen, 10 cattle, 42 sheep, and 11 swine. 1860 lists Barnett and sons as owning only 60 acres, valued at $300.

- **Bauder, Ezra**: His wife was Julia. Bauder was the principle of Culpeper County's Secondary School at Brandy Station. Later he was professor at the Wheatley Academy in Brandy Station. In 1856, Charles Urquhart deeded him 170 acres on the Rappahannock River for the development project of Rappahannock City. The property was part of Urquhart's land venture. 1870 tax records show that Bauder owned 1400 acres. This may have been confused with the rest of Urquhart's property. He lost the original 170 acres for back taxes and in 1876, W. D Foster purchased it from the treasurer for $85.00. Foster then deeded 79 acres back to Bauder to live on. 1880 tax records show that Bauder still owned 75 acres. He sold the land to the Powhatan Mining Company in 1890 after he moved to Laurinburg, North Carolina. (DB 18-339, 342, 343; DB 23-488; *See Ellis Ford Chapter, Rappahannock City*)

- **Beard, John**: 1880 tax records show that he owned 48 unimproved acres, valued at $200, 1 milk cow, 1 cow and 1 swine. Married Margaret Childs. Buried in the Richardsville Methodist Cemetery.

- **Bell, Richard**: His farm was located down River Beach Road, off of Route 619. River Beach Road is a private drive just across from Beach Road, Route 743. Garden's 1876 map shows that he owned 276 acres. 1860 tax records show that he owned 282 acres, 141 of them improved, valued at $915, 4 horses, 5 milk cows, 50 sheep, 5 cattle, and 31 swine. In 1870, he still had 282 acres, 100 of them improved, valued at $2,108, with 4 horses, 6 milk cows, but only 12 sheep and 8 swine. By 1880, he had 7 horses, 8 milk cows, and 35 swine. The farm value was $2,160. (*See Bells Ford Chapter*)

- **Bell, George W.**: b. 1843?. Son of Richard Bell. George was reported living in or near Fredericksburg in 1908. (*See Company E, 13th Virginia Infantry, Appendix IV and Bells Ford Chapter*)

- **Bell, William T.**: Son of Richard Bell. Conscripted into Confederate army, 4/27/1863 at Culpeper Court House. (*See Company B, 13th Virginia Infantry, Appendix IV and Bells Ford Chapter*)

- **Bradshaw, Mrs.**: Campbell's 1863 Civil War map shows her residence located at Culpeper Mine.

- **Childs**: Schedler's Civil War map shows a Child's residence near Skinkers Ford, on the Rapidan River.

- **Childs, Francis**: 1860 tax records show that he owned 724 acres, 500 of them improved, valued at $10,080, 2 horses, 3 milk cows, 4 work oxen, 6 cattle, and 2 swine.

- **Childs, George**: Lived off the north side of Route 610, just west of Curtis Mill Road, on a ridge. 1880 tax records show that he owned 14 acres, valued at $50. He was named as a county registrar for the WWI draft board in June, 1917. In 1918, he inherited 93 acres (originally part of Peachwood) from Emma Childs. (DB 60-420; Scheel, *Culpeper, A Virginia County's History*, p. 329)

- **Childs (Hall), Mary**: b. 1834 - d. 1914. Wife of Alexander Hall.

- **Childs, W.**: Campbell's 1863 Civil War map locates a Child's residence on the north side of Route 610, about a quarter mile west of Hazel Run. Schedler's 1863 Civil War map labels the house as W. Childs. It appears to be the same area as John Weedon's farm. 1870 tax records show that he owned 40 acres, valued at $240.

- **Chancellor, James C.**: Richardsville's postmaster 1/5/1846.

- **Colbert, A. L.**: Garden's 1876 map shows the property as 95 acres located near the Jerry's Flats section of the Rapidan River. Scheel's map of Culpeper County locates him on the south side of Middle Run.

- **Coppage, R. E.**: Worked for H. S. Marean as a teamster/logger. He served in the army during WWI. After the war he lived behind the Oakland Baptist Church's cemetery on Route 610. Robert Coppage is buried in the Oakland Baptist cemetery. Scheel's History of Culpeper County states that he was drafted in 1917 (p. 329).

- **Curtis, Douglas**: Son of Jim Curtis. At one time he got into a fight with Martin Vanburean Smith over a girl and was tried in Rodger's Store by Robert Allison. Allison fined him $10. At one time he lived in the Staunton/Barnett house. (*See Martin Smith*)

- **Curtis, Frank**: 1860 tax records show that he owned 90 acres, 60 of them improved, valued at $800, 2 horses, 1 milk cow, 2 cattle, and 1 swine.

- **Curtis, Jim**: Lived at the southwest corner of Jennings Road and Route 610.

- **Curtis, John F.**: 1870 tax records show that he owned 82 acres, 57 of them improved, valued at $525, 1 horse, 1 mule, 2 milk cows, and 2 swine. Garden's 1876 map shows the property as 75 acres at the end of Jennings Road. Scheel's map of Culpeper County locates his house on a bluff overlooking the Rapidan River just downstream of the Locust Hill Plantation. (*See Company E, 13th Virginia Infantry, Appendix IV*)

- **Curtis, Jesse**: 1870 tax records show that he owned 292 acres, 242 of them improved, valued at $800, 2 horses, 1 mule, 2 milk cows, and 2 swine. Garden's 1876 map shows the property as 100 acres near Skinkers Ford on the Rapidan River. (*See Company E, 13th Virginia Infantry, Appendix IV*)

- **Curtis, (Hall) Nancy**: b. 1802 - d. ? Married Daniel Hall.

- **Curtis, Susan**: 1850 tax records show that she owned 750 acres, all 750 of them improved, valued at $3,000, 2 milk cows, 2 cattle, and 1 swine. 1870 tax records show that she owned 292 acres, 100 of them improved, valued at $1,450, 2 milk cows, 2 cattle, and 1 swine.

- **Curtis, Walter**: Schedler's Civil War map identifies a W. Curtis house on Route 610, just across the intersection with Jennings Road. Garden's 1876 map confirms the property as W. Curtis with 136 acres. 1870 tax records show that he owned 136 acres, 25 of them improved, valued at $680, 1 horse, 1 milk cow, 1 sheep, and 9 swine. (*See Company E, 13th Virginia Infantry, Appendix IV*)

- **Daverson, Lillie**: 1880 tax records show that she owned 450 acres, 50 of them improved, valued at $2,000, 2 horses, 2 mules, 8 milk cows, 4 cattle, 35 swine.

- **Downey, Darby**: Garden's 1876 map shows the property as 561 acres. It was located across from the present day Salvation Army Camp. The residence is also identified on a Schedler's Civil War map. 1870 tax records show that he owned three tracts of land, one 358 acres, one 140 acres, and one 31 acres, all valued at $2,045, 3 horses, 5 milk cows, 2 work oxen, 5 cattle, and 1 swine. He may have had a son named William. (*See Company E, 13th Virginia Infantry, Appendix IV*)

- **Ellington, Virginia**: The Ellington's lived off Beach Road (Route 743). 1870 tax records show that she owned 49 acres, 19 of them improved, valued at $134, 2 milk cows, 4 cattle, and 5 swine. 1880 tax records show that she owned 52 acres, 24 of them improved, valued at $200, 2 milk cows, 4 cattle, and 5 swine. She may have been John Ellington's wife. (*See John Ellington, Company E, 13th Virginia Infantry, Appendix IV*)

- **Ellis, Lewis**: 1860 tax records show that he owned 1,100 acres in Culpeper County, 500 of them improved, valued at $10,800, and 200 acres in Fauquier County, 185 of them improved, valued at $9,000. He had 20 horses, 8 milk cows, 60 cattle, 125 sheep, and 150 swine. Garden's 1876 map shows the property in Culpeper County as 449 acres. It later became West Marganna. Ellis died in 1869. (*See Ellis Ford Chapter, Mills; Gold Mines*)

- **Eley, Edward**: His farm was located just north of Orchard Farm. 1850 tax records show he owned 138 acres, 133 of them improved, valued at $1,281, 2 horses, 2 milk cows, 3 cattle, 2 work oxen, 50 sheep, and 60 swine. 1880 tax records show that he owned 170 acres with only 15 acres improved, 5 horses, 4 milk cows, 4 cattle, and 2 swine. (*See Skinkers Ford Chapter, 1864; Post Civil War*)

- **Embrey, Eddie**: His house is still standing on the south side of Route 610 next to Oakland Baptist Church. He built in 1914/15 and was a carpenter and mail carrier. In the 1920s, a small store was located on the northwest corner of the property.

- **Embrey, Joesph**: Chief prospector of the Embrey Mine near Elys Ford. The only pre Civil War mine not to be incorporated. (Scheel, *History of Culpeper County*, p. 128; *See Gold Mines, Appendix II*)

- **Field, Daniel**: His house site is off White Rock Road and the foundation remains. (*KIA, See Company E, 13th Virginia Infantry, Appendix IV*)

- **Field, Henry**: 1870 tax records show that he owned 250 acres, 100 of them improved, valued at $1540, 1 horse, 2 milk cows, 2 cattle, and 3 swine.

- **Field, James R.**: Garden's 1876 map shows the property as 121 acres on the east side of Mill Run. The property is also found on Campbell's 1863 Civil War map. Scheel's map of Culpeper County locates his house just across from the Field's Mill. 1870 tax records show that he owned two tracts of land, one with 700 acres, 100 of them improved, valued at $3,000, and the other with 193 acres, non cultivated, valued at $960, 3 horses, 3 milk cows, 2 cattle, and 6 swine. 1880 tax records show that he owned 301 acres, 300 of them unimproved, valued at $800, 4 milk cows, 4 cattle, and 8 swine. (*See Company E, 13th Virginia Infantry, Appendix IV*)

- **Field, Joseph**: 1850 tax records show that he owned 800 acres, 300 of them improved, 10 horses, 2 mules, 5 milk cows, 4 oxen, 18 cattle, 50 sheep, and 25 swine.

- **Field, Joesph R.**: Married Lula Hall. Richardsville store owner. Postmaster of Richardsville from 1889 to 1913. (Scheel, *History of Culpeper County*, p. 128; *See Joseph Field's Store, Appendix III*)

- **Field, Lucy Ann**: 1850 tax records show that she owned 250 acres, 100 of them improved, valued at $2,000, 2 horses, 3 milk cows, 5 cattle, and 15 swine.

- **Fields, Thomas**: Garden's 1876 map shows that he owned 218 acres on the Rappahannock River, upstream of Rodger's property. 1870 tax records show that he owned 213 acres, 150 of them improved, valued at $1,526, 2 horses, 2 milk cows, 7 cattle, and 10 swine. 1880 tax records show that he owned 170 acres, 55 of them improved, valued at $500, 2 horses, 2 milk cows, 2 cattle, and 12 swine. (*See Company E, 13th VA Infantry, Appendix IV*)
-
- **Field, William D.**: Nominated in 1859 to act as Captain of the 5th Regiment, Virginia Militia. Garden's 1876 map shows that he lived upstream of Thomas Field's property. 1870 tax records show that he owned 800 acres, 400 of them improved, valued at $6,100, 3 horses, 4 milk cows, 4 work oxen, 15 cattle, and 8 swine. 1880 tax records show that he owned 420 acres, 180 of them improved, valued at $2,500, 3 horses, 1 mule, 4 milk cows, 12 cattle, 10 sheep, and 35 swine. (Scheel's, *History of Culpeper County*, p. 172)

- **Field, W. H.**: 1880 tax records show that he owned 8 acres, 2 of them improved, valued at $100, 2 milk cows, 2 cattle, and 8 swine.

- **Foster, Mary J.**: Richardsville's postmaster 3/11/1868.

- **Foster, Warrenton D.**: 1870 tax records show that he owned 100 acres, 75 of them improved, valued at $1,000, 1 horse, 7 milk cows, 4 cattle, 16 swine. 1880 tax records show that he owned 96 unimproved acres, valued at $300, plus another 125 acres with 35 of them improved, valued at $1,000, 2 horses, 2 milk cows, 2 oxen, and 4 cattle. Foster built a house and store across from the present Richardsville Store, around 1850. The store and house were across the road from each other. The house still stands and is presently owned by Fred Ricker. In 1871, he donated land for the Richardsville Methodist Church. He was Richardsville's postmaster in 1873. Foster was a carpenter, wheelwright, storekeeper, and investor in local property. (Scheel, *Culpeper, A Virginia County's History*, p. 261; *Ibid.*, p. 270; *See Richardsville Stores, Appendix III*)

- **Gatewood, Martha**: b. 1828 - d. after 1900. 1880 tax records show that she owned 1 acre, valued at $40. She was Oswald Pemberton's housekeeper and niece. In 1874, upon his death, Oswald willed her his house and household items. The house was located on the south side of Route 610, next to Hazel Run.

- **Gathright, John**: Smith's Tavern (Richardsville) postmaster 12/15/1828.

- **Green, Britten Barbee**: b. 1854 - d. 1929. Married Ida Hall. He had a house near "*Locust Hill*" on a bluff, just east of Lick Run. The house burned down in the late 1930s.

- **Grims, C**: His property was located on the Rappahannock River upstream of John Pemberton's farm. Garden's 1876 map shows it as 617 acres.

- **Hall, Alexander C**.: b. 1828 - d. 1903. Married Mary Childs. He was the son of Daniel Hall. Garden's 1876 map shows the property as 120 acres on the Rapidan River. It was also the location of Halls Ford. Eugene Scheel's Historic Site Survey states that in 1871 Daniel Hall built a house for his son, Alexander. The house still stands at the end of Halls Road. 1880 tax records show that Alexander still owned the 120 acres, 50 of them improved, valued at $500, 3 horses, 5 milk cows, 4 cattle, and 14 swine.

- **Hall, Amy**: 1850 tax records show that she owned 400 acres, 300 of them improved, valued at $8,000, 5 horses, 7 milk cows, 4 work oxen, 12 cattle, 47 sheep, and 31 swine.

- **Hall, Dr. Arthur J.**: b. 1874 - d. 1948. Married Fonce Smith. Son of Alexander Hall. He was a Professor at a University in Texas. Dr. Hall came to Richardsville each summer to visit for a few weeks and stayed with his brother, Bradley, at the Hall Farm. He drove a Pierce Arrow automobile which he would leave at the Richardsville Store because he did not want it to get dirty driving to the farm.

- **Hall, Bradley**: b. 1869 - d. 1945. Married Almeda Love. Operated the Richardsville Country Store.

- **Hall, Charles**: b. 1870 - d. 1960. Married Elizabeth Utz. Son of Alexander Hall.

- **Hall, Daniel**: b. 1798 - d. 1875. Married Nancy Curtis. 1850 tax records show that he owned 550 acres on the Rapidan River, 300 of them improved, valued at $3,260, 6 horses, 5 milk cows, 3 work oxen, 15 cattle, 15 sheep, and 5 swine. 1860 tax records show that he owned 640 acres, 240 of them improved, 5 horses, 7 milk cows, 4 work oxen, 9 cattle, 24 sheep, and 20 swine. It was the location of Halls Ford. The Sketch of the Operations of the Army of the Potomac and Koeber's Civil War map identifies the Daniel's house.

- **Hall (Green), Ida**: b. 1864 - d. 1926. Daughter of Alexander Hall. Wife of Brittan Green.

- **Hall, Lula Davis**: b. 1862 - d. 1928. Daughter of Alexander Hall. Wife of Joseph Fields. After Joseph died, she gave the Richardsville store to her brother, Bradley Hall.

- **Hall, Mattie Larkin**: b. 1859 - d.1931. Married O. G. Hall.

- **Hall, Philip**: 1860 tax records show that he owned 290 acres, none cultivated, valued at $1,099, no livestock.

- **Hall, Sanford F.**: b. 1866 - d.? Married Laura Smith. Son of Alexander Hall. He was a mail carrier.

- **Hall, (Weedon), Virginia**: b. 1840 - d. 1928. Married Isaac Weedon. Buried in the Hall cemetery. Her grave marker is the only one readable.

- **Hall, William**: 1850 tax records show that he owned 1,100 acres, 150 of them improved, valued at $4,400, 1 milk cow, and 8 swine.

- **Hardins**: Not located on any map, but most likely near Hardin's Mill and Hardins Ford.

- **Harding**: Sketch of the Operations of the Army of the Potomac identifies the property on the north side of 610 at Elys Ford, now River Hill Farm area.

- **Harding, Richard**: May be the Harding above. 1870 tax records show that he owned 125 acres, not cultivated, 25 of them improved, valued at $650, 2 horses, 1 milk cow, 2 work oxen, 4 cattle, 4 sheep, and 15 swine.

- **Hickerson, J.**: Schedler's Civil War map and the Sketch of the Operations of the Army of the Potomac identifies the residence on Route 610, near Elys Ford, across the road from the W. Child's residence. Captain Koeber's Civil War map locates the property on the same side of the road as W. Child's residence, next to Hazel Run. It appears to be the same location as John Weedon's.

- **Hickerson, W.**: Garden's 1876 map shows the property as 164 acres located near Oswald Pemberton's.

- **Heflin, John**: Sketch of the Operations of the Army of the Potomac identifies his house about half-way down Ellis Ford Road. Heflin was a overseer for Lewis Ellis's slaves. 1870 tax records show that he owned 800 acres, 300 of them improved, valued at $8,000, 1 horse, 3 milk cows, 2 work oxen, and 5 sheep. This may have been obtained by the death of Lewis Ellis the year before. 1880 tax records show that he owned 600 acres with 300 of them improved, valued at $4,000, 7 horses, 4 milk cows, 15 cattle, and 64 sheep. 1880 tax records also show that he owned another 600 acres, 300 of them improved, 4 milk cows, 18 cattle, 114 sheep, and 11 swine. (*See Company E, 13th Virginia Infantry, Appendix IV*)

- **Herndon & Ellis**: 1860 tax records show that they owned 1,000 acres, 200 of them improved, valued at $2,500, 1 horse, 3 milk cows, 4 oxen, and 7 swine. 1860 tax records show an additional 500 acres, which may have been in conjunction with the Urquharts because Herndon and Urquhart are listed together. This may have been a gold mining operation that later became the Cromarty Mines. Garden's 1876 map shows the property as 560 acres off of Route 619 east of Orchard Farm.

- **Humphreys, Captain Andrew Jackson**: b. 1826 or 28. Son of Captain Thomas Humphreys. Living in Alexandria, Virginia in 1860. Joined the 17th Virginia Infantry as Lieutenant. He died at the Battle of Williamsburg, May 5, 1862.

- **Humphreys, Ann M.** : b. 1803 - d. 1886. Daughter of Captain Thomas Humphreys. Married William Thomas Jefferson Richards.

- **Humphreys, Bettie Lewis**; b. 1824 - d. 1899. Daughter of Captain Thomas Humphreys. 1870 tax records show that she owned 160 acres, 100 of them improved, valued at $700, 1 horse, 2 milk cows, 4 cattle, and 6 swine. 1880 tax records show that she still owned 160 acres, 15 of them improved, valued at $500, 2 milk cows, 2 cattle, and 2 swine.

- **Humphreys, Catherine A.**: b. ca 1815 - d. 1881. Daughter of Captain Thomas Humphreys. 1860 tax records show that she owned 114 acres, 100 of them improved, valued at $600, 2 horses, 2 milk cows, and 1 swine.

- **Humphreys, Flodorado**: b. ca. 1816 - d. 1877. Son of Captain Thomas Humphreys. Married Judith Harris. He was the Richardsville postmaster 1/7/1853. In 1857, Flodorado inherited a 39 acre lot of the Thomas Humphrey's estate off of Route 683 just west of Oak Shade, and built a house there. Just before the Civil War he moved to Fauquier County, near the Wycoff Mines. He was superintendent of the Liberty Mines. He may also been involved with the Franklin Mines. 1860 tax records show that he owned 600 acres in Fauquier County, 200 of them improved, valued at $6,000, 7 horses, 5 milk cows, 1 cow, and 5 swine. He died of stomach cancer and is buried in the same grave as his wife, as they died only a few days apart. Sometime before 1870 he sold the 39 acre lot and house on Route 683 to Thomas Pemberton. Thomas later deeded the property off of Route 683 to his daughter Lucy. The house stood until the 1980's, then fell in upon itself. The last residents were the Brook sisters during the 1950s.

- **Humphreys, Isabella Miller**: b. 1800? - d. 1870. Daughter of Captain Thomas Humphreys. Married John Pemberton, 1820. Lived at *"Oak Shade"*. (*See Skinkers Ford Chapter, Post Civil War*)

- **Humphreys, Jeff**: 1860 tax records show that he owned 39 acres.

- **Humphreys, John B.**: b. 1811 - d. 1884. Son of Captain Thomas Humphreys. Married Susan Jane Childs. Richardsville postmaster 12/23/1847. He is buried in back of Oakland Baptist Church. His initials JBH are on the fieldstone marking his grave. His house is next to Fred Ricker's (W. D. Foster's) house across the road from the Richardsville Store. Eugene Scheel's Historic Site Survey states the house was built in 1843 and a second story added by Sanford Martin in the early 1900s. It is the oldest surviving structure in Richardsville. 1850 tax records show that he owned 500 acres, 70 of them improved, valued at $2,500, 3 horses, 3 milk cows, 4 cattle, 18 sheep and 134 swine. 1860 tax records show that he still owned 550 acres, 180 of them improved, valued at $3,750, 6 horses, 3 milk cows, 6 cattle, and 11 swine. 1880 tax records show that he owned 150 acres, 25 of them improved, valued at $750, 3 horses, 2 milk cows, 3 cattle, 222 sheep, and 16 swine.

- **Humphreys, James Richards P.**: b. ca 1800. Son of Captain Thomas Humphreys. 1880 tax records show that he owned 325 acres, 25 of them improved, valued at $1,000, 3 milk cows and 4 cattle.

- **Humphreys, Lucy**: b. ca 1825- d. after 1876. Daughter of Captain Thomas Humphreys.

- **Humphreys, Malvina S.**: b. ca 1810 - d. after 1876. Daughter of Captain Thomas Humphreys. 1870 tax records show that she owned 120 acres, 30 of them improved, valued at $600, 2 milk cows, 2 cattle, and 2 swine.

- **Humphreys, S. E.**: 1880 tax records show that he owned 150 acres, 10 of them improved, valued at $360, 1 milk cow, 1 cow, and 2 swine.

- **Humphreys, Captain (Colonel) Thomas**: b. 1765 - d. 1848. Married Elizabeth Richards, daughter of William Richards. They had 14 children. He owned a 500 acre plantation called "*Locust Hill*" located on the Rapidan River, one mile south of the fire tower. The residence is identified as Col. Humphreys on various Civil War maps. Some earlier records list him as Captain Humphreys. 1870 tax records show his estate as 500 acres, 50 of them improved, valued at $1,500.

- **Humphreys, Thomas Jefferson**: b. 1809. Son of Captain Thomas Humphreys. Married Lucretia Jones.

- **Humphreys, William Thomas**: b. 1814. Son of Captain Thomas Humphreys. He lived at the homeplace, "*Locust Hill*". 1850 tax records show that he owned 600 acres, 300 of them improved, valued at $300, 5 horses. 5 milk cows, 10 cattle, 20 sheep, and 10 swine. He died 7/31/1863 at Point Lookout Prison and is buried there.

- **Jennings**: Garden's 1876 map shows the property as 104 acres at Skinkers Ford, on the Rapidan River. Sketch of the Operations of the Army of The Potomac identifies a Jennings shop at the same location.

- **Jennings, Edward**: Garden's 1876 map shows the property as 75 acres between Route 610 and the Jennings tract at Skinkers Ford, on the Rapidan River. The location appears to be about half way down the present Curtis Mill Road. 1870 tax records show that he owned 75 acres, 60 of them improved, 1 horse, 1 milk cow, 2 cattle, and 1 swine. 1880 tax records show that he owned 73 acres, 20 of them improved, valued at $1,000, 3 milk cows, 3 cattle, and 2 swine. (*See Company E, 13th Virginia Infantry, Appendix IV*)

- **Jennings, George (Tom)**: 1850 census records list him as a lock keeper on the Rappahannock River Canal System. He held Union sympathies during the Civil War. On 7/15/1861 he refused to join the militia and was arrested, tried, and released a week later due to poor health. 1860 tax records show that he owned 183 acres, 125 of them improved, valued at $1,850, 1 horse, 5 milk cows, 2 cattle, and 5 swine. 1870 tax records show that he owned two tracts of land, 117 acres, 40 of them improved, valued at $ 909, and the other tract of 23 acres, 4 of them improved, valued at $240. (Scheel, *Culpeper, A Virginia County's History*, p. 149; Sunderland, *Seasons of War*, p. 70)

- **Jennings, Joseph**: 1860 tax records show that he owned 105 acres, 54 of them improved, valued at $1,500, 3 horses, 4 milk cows, 4 cattle, 8 sheep, and 5 swine. Most likely the Jennings listed above in Garden's 1876 map with 104 acres.

- **Jennings, Susan**: Her house is located about half way down Curtis Mill Road, Route 733, on the right. Scheel's Historic Site Survey states that it is thought to be built around 1840 and to be the oldest house still standing in the Richardsville area. The house may have been built for William Curtis, because it was all Curtis land until divided in 1848. Susan Jennings moved into it in 1848 and was the wife of Fred Embrey. The residence is also identified on various Civil War maps.

- **Johnson, Larman G.**: He was the owner of the Powhatan Mining Company. (*See Ellis Ford Chapter, Gold Mines and Appendix II, Gold Mines*)

- **Johnson**: Garden's 1876 map shows that a Johnson owned 50 acres on the south side of Route 610 at Elys Ford. The location is also identified on Campbell's 1863 Civil War map. It is now the Eagle Hill Horse Farm.

- **Jones, J and C**: 1850 tax records show that they owned 800 acres, 200 of them improved, valued at $3,000, 2 horses, 2 milk cows, 4 cattle, 6 sheep, and 15 swine.

- **Jones, John R.**: 1850 tax records show that he owned 103 acres, 70 of them improved, valued at $417, 3 horses, 5 milk cows, 3 cattle, and 11 swine.

- **Jones, Roy**: 1850 tax records show that he owned 54 acres, valued at $1,000, 1 horse, 1 milk cow, and 17 swine.

- **Jones, William**: 1850 tax records show that he owned 200 acres, 50 of them improved, valued at $800, 4 milk cows, 4 cattle, 45 sheep, and 29 swine. He lived on Captain Thomas Humphrey's "Locust Hill" property before and just after the Civil War. Near Thomas Humphrey's house were several houses on the ridge overlooking the Rapidan River, and the Jones house may have been one of them.

- **Jones, William T.**: 1870 tax records show that he owned 35 acres, 25 of them improved, valued at $200, 2 milk cows, 3 cattle, 2 sheep, and 8 swine. (*See Company E, 13th Virginia Infantry, Appendix IV*)

- **Kemp, George**: 1880 tax records show that he owned 10 acres, 1 improved, valued at $200, and 2 swine.

- **Kemper**: Garden's 1876 map shows the property as 396 acres near Southard's Crossing (*fire tower*).

- **Kemper, Henry N.**: 1850 tax records show he owned 500 acres, 300 of them improved, valued at $3,500, 3 horses, 1 mule, 5 milk cows, 2 work oxen, 30 cattle, 215 sheep, and 40 swine. 1870 tax records show that he owned 84 acres, 68 of them improved, valued at $1,540, 1 horse, 1 milk cow, and 3 swine.

- **Kemper, M. J.**: 1880 tax records show that he owned 13 acres, 1 improved, valued at $100, 2 milk cows, and 1 cow.

- **Kemper, William**: 1850 tax records show that he owned 1,030 acres, 650 of them improved, valued at $5,000, 5 horses, 2 milk cows, 4 work oxen, 28 cattle, 19 sheep, and 26 swine.

- **Love, Almeda**: Wife of Bradley Hall.

- **Love, W. B.**: 1880 tax records show that he owned 303 acres, 6 of them improved, valued at $1,200, 2 horses, 1 milk cow, and 2 work oxen.

- **Marean, Harold S.**: In the first half of the twentieth century he owned several tracts of land in the area. Marean had a house built at Orchard Farm, and the foundation still remains. He is remembered as wearing high riding boots that laced up. Harold moved to Warrenton and then to Florida.

- **Martin, L. W.**: 1880 tax records show that he owned 39 acres, 8 of them improved, valued at $100, 2 horses, 3 milk cows, 3 cattle, and 7 swine.

- **Martin, Martha**: Mother of Robert Martin. She had three children by Lewis Ellis. Ellis built her a house on Waugh Run, near Skinkers Ford. 1870 census records show that she was 39 years old, which meant that she was 15 when she had Robert Martin. (*See Ellis Ford Chapter, Mills*)

- **Martin, Pete**: Son of Martha Martin. He died when kicked in the head by a horse while working the Powhatan Gold Mines. Buried next to Martha in the Oakland Baptist Cemetery.

- **Martin, Robert**: b. 1846 - d. 1925. Son of Martha Martin. Married Eliza Pemberton. Lived on the Rappahannock River off of Route 683. Robert Martin's house is one of the few houses that remains from the 1800's. It is also the site of Skinkers/Martins Ford. The property is now the Rappahannock River Campground. 1870 tax records show that he owned 465 acres. His father, Lewis Ellis, died the previous year, and Robert evidently ended up with some of his property. 1880 tax records show that he owned 39 acres at Skinkers Ford, all unimproved, valued at $150, 2 horses, 1 milk cow, 1 cow, and 10 swine. He eventually purchased two adjoining 39 acre lots. (*See Skinkers Ford Chapter, Post Civil War*)

- **Martin, Sanford**: b. 1868 - d.1934. Son of Robert Martin. Purchased John Humphrey's house at Richardsville in 1904 and added a second story. He worked in the Culpeper Gold Mine and the various logging/sawmill operations in the area. He was to move into the cottage at Robert Martin's farm after he got married, but unexpectedly showed up with a different bride.

- **Martin, Murrey (Buck)**: His house is located on the left side of Route 683, just before Robert Martin's property, and directly in front of Flodorado Humphrey's house. Scheel's Historic Site Survey states the property was sold to Murrey Martin in 1882, and he built a house that started out as a saw mill shanty. James Boals purchased the property in 1900 and enlarged the house.

- **Mastin, James**: 1850 tax records show that he owned 300 acres, 210 of them improved, valued at $4,500, 5 horses, 4 milk cows, 6 cattle, and 26 swine. He lived near Fields Ford on the Rappahannock River. Mastin was responsible for canal maintenance upstream of Fields Ford. In 1857, he died at age 30 after working on the canal in the cold weather. (Scheel, *Culpeper, A Virginia County's History*, pp. 149-150)

- **Maupin, Horace**: Obtained *"Peach Grove"* from Thomas Pemberton when he married his daughter, Minnie. The house and farm were located at the end of Route 683. (*See Skinkers Ford Chapter, Post Civil War*)

- **McConchie, John W.**: 1870 tax records show that he owned 20 acres, 5 of them improved, valued at $600, 3 milk cows, 2 cattle, and 3 swine.

- **McChonchie, Marvin, P.**: His house is located on Route 610 across from the Oakland Baptist Church. Scheel's Historic Site Survey states the house appears to be built in the early 1900s. Marvin McConchie lived there until 1930, then the Beach family purchased it. The store next to the house was built and operated by the Beach's for about a decade. (*See Beach's Store, Appendix III*)

- **Miller, B. D.**: Garden's 1876 map shows that he lived on, or near Gill's Run Creek and owned 113 acres. He may have been related to Simon Miller. (*See Miller's Mill, Appendix I*)

- **Miller, Simon**: Original owner of the land between the Rappahannock and Rapidan Rivers at *"The Neck"*. His daughter, Eliza, married William Richards, thus Simon gave the land to William and his daughter. (*See Richards Ford Chapter, Settlement*)

- **Miller, William**: 1850 tax records show that he owned 188 acres, 175 of them improved, valued at $1,178, 2 horses, 5 milk cows, 2 work oxen, 7 cattle, 7 sheep, and 26 swine.

- **Miller, W. H.**: 1880 tax records show that he owned 100 acres, with 30 acres improved, valued at $800, 1 horse, 3 milk cows, 2 work oxen, 2 cattle, and 15 swine. He may be the same William Miller listed above.

- **Newby, E. A.**: 1880 tax records show that he owned 640 acres, 490 of them improved, 3 horses, 10 milk cows, 17 cattle, 61 sheep, and 2 swine.

- **Newby, Mary**: b.1765 - d.1815. Wife of Larkin Pemberton of *"Orchard Farm"*.

- **Newby, Henry**: 1850 tax records show that he owned 246 acres, 150 of them improved, valued at $2,957, 5 horses, 3 milk cows, 5 cattle, 14 sheep, and 20 swine.

- **Newby, R. C.**: Garden's 1876 map shows his property as 182 (102?) acres at the same location as the Harding house, on the north side of 610 at Elys Ford.

- **Newby, Major William P.**: b.1785- d.1847. 1850 tax records show that he owned 500 acres, 300 of them improved, valued at $7,500, 9 horses, 5 milk cows, 4 work oxen, 8 cattle, 14 sheep, 20 swine.

- **Pemberton, Bettie**: 1880 tax records show that she owned 110 acres, 35 of them improved, valued at $800, 4 horses, 2 milk cows, and 2 cattle.

- **Pemberton, Eliza Delilah**: b. 1839 - d.1920. Wife of Robert Martin (*See Skinkers Ford Chapter*, *Post Civil War*)

- **Pemberton, Mary A.**: 1870 tax records show that she owned 102 acres, 50 of them improved, valued at $612, 3 milk cows, 2 work oxen, and 4 cattle. 1880 tax records show that she owned 110 acres, 35 of them improved, valued at $700, no livestock.

- **Pemberton, J. O.**: 1880 tax records show that he owned 550 unimproved acres, valued at $2,000, 4 milk cows, 6 cattle and 12 swine.

- **Pemberton, John**: b. 1799 - d. 1870. Married Isabella Humphreys. He owned 150 acres on the Rappahannock River called "*Oak Shade*", next to Robert Martin's property. 1850 tax records show that he owned 1 horse, 2 milk cows, 5 cattle, 16 sheep, and 31 swine. 1860 tax records show that he owned 110 improved acres, valued at $550, 1 horse, 4 milk cows, 2 work oxen, 8 cattle, 7 sheep, and 8 swine. (*See Skinkers Ford Chapter, Post Civil War*)

- **Pemberton, (Humphreys) Isabella**: b. 1800-1803? - d. 1873? Wife of John Pemberton. 1870 tax records show that she owned 150 acres, 110 of them improved, valued at $750, 3 milk cows, 2 work oxen, 2 cattle, and 3 swine.

- **Pemberton, Larkin**: ca. b. 1767- d. 5/22/1822. His first wife was Mary Newby and his second wife was Behethelon Wheatley. He owned "*Orchard Farm*" located off of Route 619 about a half mile across from the intersection with Route 683. The house was built around 1802. It is also the location of the Pemberton Cemetery. (*See Skinkers Ford Chapter, Post Civil War*). Larkin owned 674 acres, and after he died his will listed 19 slaves. His property was divided among his children. Later in the 1840s, twelve slaves were divided between his daughters Mary and Kitty (Catherine). They are as follows:

Davy, $1.00
Fanny and child, $100.00
Diana, $600.00
Washington $800.00
David, $400.00
Larkin, $200.00

Eliza, $450.00
Henry, $574.00
Polly, $600.00
John, $500.00
Juliet, $300.00

- **Pemberton, Lucy**: Daughter of Thomas Pemberton. Lived in Flodorado Humphrey's house after her father Thomas Pemberton purchased it. (*See Skinkers Ford Chapter, Post Civil War*)

- **Pemberton, Malvina S**.: b. 1829 - d. 1906. Daughter of John Pemberton. She lived at *"Oak Shade"* until her death.

- **Pemberton, Minnie**: b. 1855 - d. 1940. Daughter of Thomas Pemberton. She married Horace Maupin and Thomas passed *"Peach Grove"* on to them.

- **Pemberton, Oswald N**.: b. 1799 - d. 1874. Never married. Owned *"Peachwood"* plantation. The location is identified on both Schedler's and Campbell's 1863 Civil War maps just south of Hazel Run, off of Route 610. His house was made of stone. 1850 tax records show that Oswald owned 1,200 acres, 400 of them improved, valued at $12,000, 13 horses, 6 milk cows, 50 cattle, 50 sheep, and 60 swine. 1860 tax records show that he owned 2,270 acres, 800 of them improved, valued at $36,550, 7 horses, 2 mules, 8 milk cows, 4 work oxen, 40 cattle, 60 sheep, and 15 swine. 1870 tax records show that he owned eight tracts of land totaling 3,551 acres, with only 650 cultivated, and valued at $17,668, 4 horses, 5 milk cows, 2 work oxen, 16 cattle, and 10 swine. He was a road commissioner from 1837 to 1840 and was on the school board for 30 years.

- **Pemberton, Sarah (Sallie) F**.: b. 1841 - d. 1910?. Lived on the corner of her fathers farm (John Pemberton), *"Oak Shade"*. (*See Skinkers Ford Chapter, Post Civil War*)

- **Pemberton, Thomas L**.: b. 1821- d. 1903. Married Ann Bullard. 1870 tax records show that he owned 135 acres, 70 of them improved, valued at $834, 1 horse, 6 milk cows, 2 cattle, 4 sheep, and 4 swine. He called it *"Peach Grove"*. 1880 tax records show that he owned 130 acres, 60 of them improved, valued at $1,000, 1 horse no livestock. (*See Skinkers Ford Chapter, Post Civil War; Company E, 13th Virginia Infantry, Appendix IV*)

- **Pemberton, William (Billy)**: b. 1836. Son of John Pemberton and brother of Thomas Pemberton. KIA during the Civil War. (*See Skinkers Ford Chapter, Post Civil War and Company E, 13th Virginia Infantry, Appendix IV*)

- **Reynolds, Robert**: His house is located in Richardsville between John Humphrey's house and the Richardsville Fire Department. It was built in 1906 by Morton Reynolds, before he moved to Texas. Robert lived there until 1937 and then Carl Eley and his wife Myrtle Walker purchased it. The large oak trees in the front yard appear to be well over 100 years old, suggesting a previous house occupied the location.

- **Richards, Kathy**: 1860 tax records show that she owned 128 improved acres, valued at $1,280, 6 horses, 7 milk cows, 1 work oxen, 7 cattle, 30 sheep, and 10 swine.

- **Richards, Benjamin**: b. 1806 - d. 1879. Son of James Richards. Married Dulcibell C. Benson. He lived near Todds Ford. Todds Ford Road is off of Route 619, just before Richards Ford. Garden's 1876 map shows his property as 300 acres. 1850 tax records also show 300 acres, valued at $2,000, 175 of them improved, 5 horses, 4 milk cows, 4 work oxen, 10 cattle, 422 sheep, and 11 swine. 1860 tax records show that he owed 314 acres, 150 of them improved, valued at $3,555, 7 horses, 1 mule, 7 milk cows, 10 cattle. 1870 tax records show that he owned 343 acres, 200 of them improved, valued at $4,000, 3 horses, 4 milk cows, 2 work oxen, 1 cow, 16 sheep, and 10 swine. 1870 tax records also show that he owned another 600 acre tract of non-cultivated land. (*See Richards Ford Chapter, Settlement*)

- **Richards, Eliza Lewis**: b. 1821- d. 1900. Daughter of Captain James Richards. Garden's 1876 map shows the property as 220 acres, located between Ben Richards and Miss M. Richards of Richards Ford. She and her sister, Mollie, inherited Point Comfort in 1857, which was 353 acres and the original Richards House. 1860 tax records show that she owned 225 acres, not cultivated, valued at $1,575, and Kathy Richards owned 128 acres, valued at $1,280. Obviously, the 353 acres were divided between them. 1880 tax records show that she still owned 225 acres, with 40 of them improved, and 20 horses. The farm value was $1,000. (*See Richards Ford Chapter, Settlement*)

- **Richards, Elizabeth**: 1870 tax records show that she owned 340 acres, 300 of them improved, valued at $2,040, 1 horse, 2 milk cows, 2 swine.

- **Richards, Elizabeth Lewis**: b. 1775 - d. 184?. Daughter of William Richards. Married Thomas Humphreys.

- **Richards, Isabella**: b. 1789 - d. 1/16/1827. Daughter of William Richards. Married Benjamin Barnett ca. 1820. (*See Ellis Ford Chapter, Mills*)

- **Richards, James**: b. 1774 - d. 1844. Son of William Richards. Married Winfred Berry Benson ca. 1799. Moved to Tennessee.

- **Richards, John J.**: 1870 tax records show that he owned 17 acres, valued at $2,500, 1 horse, and 3 cows.

- **Richards, John Royal**: b. 1856 - d. 1906. Son of Benjamin Richards. His house was located on the north side of Route 619 about one mile before Richards Ford. The house was burned down in the 1980s because it was unsafe. Brick porch pillers remain at the house site.

- **Richards, Mollie M.**: b. 1822 - d. 1903. Daughter of Captain James Richards. She and her sister, Elizainherited Point Comfort in 1857, which was 353 acres and the original Richards House. The house was torn down in the 1980s because it was considered unsafe. (*See Richards Ford Chapter, Settlement*)

- **Richards, Samuel I.**: b. 4/24/1837 - d. 1/13/1906. Son of Benjamin Richards. Buried in the family cemetery at Richards Ford. His gravestone reads "*A True Confederate Soldier*".

- **Richards, Captain William**: b. 1755 - d. 1817. Married Eliza Miller, daughter of Simon Miller, in 1773. They were in turn given the land of "*The Neck*". (*See Richards Ford Chapter, Settlement*)

- **Richards, William**: 1860 tax records show that he owned 900 acres, 600 of them improved, none cultivated, valued at $9,600. 1880 tax records show that he owned 510 acres, 490 of them unimproved, valued at $1,500. Owned a stud race horse named Alfred. (Scheel, *Culpeper, A Virginia County's History*, p. 202; *See Richards Ford Chapter, Settlement*)

- **Richards, William Thomas Jefferson**: b. 1801- d. 1886. Son of Captain James Richards. Married Ann Humphreys, daughter of Captain Thomas Humphreys, in 1827. He was postmaster of Richardsville 1831 -1835. He moved to Texas sometime after 1842. 1860 tax records show that he still owned 249 acres near Richardsville, 157 of them improved, none cultivated. (*See Richards Ford Chapter, Settlement*)

- **Rodgers, James Sr.**: Purchased 180 acres at Rogers Ford in 1827. (*See Rogers Ford Chapter, Settlement*)

- **Rodgers, James F.**: 1850 tax records show that he owned 200 acres, 100 of them improved, valued at $3,000, 2 horses, 3 milk cows, 6 cattle, and 30 swine. (*See Rogers Ford Chapter, Settlement*)

- **Rodgers, Welford N.**: Garden's 1876 map shows that he and James F. owned 150 acres at Rodgers Ford. 1870 tax records show that Welford owned 180 acres, 60 of them improved, valued at $1,080, 2 horses, 5 milk cows, 5 cattle, and 4 swine. (*See Rogers Ford Chapter, Settlement*)

- **Smith Farm**: Richardsville was originally called Smith's Tavern. The farm was located on the north side of Route 610, about a mile east of Richardsville.

- **Smith (Hall), Almeda**: Correction Almeda Love, Wife of Bradley Hall.

- **Smith (Hall), Fonce**: Correction Fonce Love, Wife of Dr. Arthur Hall.

- **Smith (Hall), Laura**: Wife of Sanford Hall.

- **Smith, James W.**: Richardsville's postmaster 1/20/1852.

- **Smith, John Minor**: He was the last resident of Rappahannock City in the early 20th century.

- **Smith, Johnson**: Richardsville postmaster 9/24/1858. (*See Company E, 13th Virginia Infantry, Appendix IV*)

- **Smith, Martin VanBuren**: Married Mollie J. in 1869. Farmer in Spotsylvania County. Died at Richardsville 6/22/31. Buried at Oakland Baptist Church, Richardsville. A local story tells of him delivering a wagon load of timber to Fredericksburg and on the next day returning with a wagon load of hay. On the return trip he set the hay and wagon on fire while lighting his pipe. Another story tells of him getting into a fight with Douglas Curtis. Evidently, Martin was saying some derogatory remarks about a local girl and Curtis took offense. Martin got beat up and the

Justice of the Peace (Robert Allison) fined Douglas $10.00 as punishment. They were tried in Foster/Roger's Store. (*See Company E, 13th Virginia Infantry, Appendix IV*)

- **Southard, H.**: Koeber's Civil War map and The Sketch of the Operations of the Army of the Potomac locates the Southard's resident just under the present day fire tower on Route 610.

- **Starkey, Lucy A.**: 1880 tax records show that she owned 90 acres, 85 of them unimproved, valued at $300, 3 milk cows, and 2 cattle.

- **Staunton, William**: Owned Staunton's Mill which he sold to William Richards prior to 1791. Eventually the mill and surrounding land became Barnett's Mill when Ben Barnett married William's daughter, Isabella. (*See Ellis Ford Chapter, Mills*)

- **Strother, J. C.**: Garden's 1876 map shows the property as 158 acres just upstream of Richards Ford.

- **Tayler, J. J.**: Garden's 1876 map shows the property as 436 acres on the Rappahannock River between Strother's and Bell's property. 1880 tax records show that he owned 430 acres, valued at $1,000, no livestock.

- **Thomas, P. L.**: Garden's 1876 map shows the property as 86 acres and the same property as the Smith Farm on the north side of Route 610. (*See Smith Farm*)

- **Thorn, William**: 1870 tax records show that he owned 324 acres. (*See Skinkers Ford Chapter, 1864*)

- **Turner, T. R.**: Garden's 1876 map shows the property as 89.5 acres located behind the Methodist church.

- **Turner, Zacharia R.**: 1870 tax records show that he owned 97 acres, 15 of them improved, valued at $300, 2 milk cows, 1 cow, and 1 swine. He deeded land for Oakland Baptist Church in 1871. (Scheel, *Culpeper, A Virginia County's History*, p. 259)

- **Tyson. Joseph**, 1880 tax records show that he owned 11 acres, valued at $100, and 4 swine. There was a Tyson lot in back of (W. D. Fosters) house. (*See Company E, 13th Virginia Infantry, Appendix IV*)

- **Urquhart, Charles and Samuel**: Garden's 1876 map shows the property estimated at 1,000 acres. 1880 tax records show that the Urquharts owned 1,230 acres, non-improved, valued at $4,000, 1 horse, and 1 milk cow. Charles was deceased by that time. (*See Ellis Ford Chapter, Rappahannock City*)

- **Walker, J.**: Sketch of the Operations of the Army of the Potomac shows J. Walker on the left side of Route 619, just prior to Walker Road. Jed Hotchiss's Civil War map of Fauquier County shows a Walker store there.

- **Walker, J. T.**: Garden's 1876 map shows J. T. Walker's farm as 270 acres on the Rappahannock River. 1850 tax records show that he owned 135 acres, 45 of them improved, valued at $870, 7 horses, 3 milk cows, 7 work oxen, 4 cattle, and 8 swine. 1860 tax records show that he owed 130 acres, 2 horses, 2 milk cows, 7 sheep, and 9 swine. 1870 tax records show that he owned 130 acres, 50 of them improved, valued at $500, 1 milk cow, 1 cow, and 1 swine. 1880 tax records show that he owned 145 acres, 55 of them improved, valued at $200, 2 horses, 3 milk cows, 3 cattle, and 7 swine. The original house, no longer standing, was on the bluff overlooking the river. It burned down from a chimney fire getting on the wooden roof shakes. Also on the bluff is a slave graveyard. A second house was built by Burruss Walker, who was a carpenter. He lived there in the 1890s. The farm stayed in the Walker family from the early 1800s until the mid 20th century.

- **Walker, Samuel**: 1850 tax records show that he owned 450 acres, 200 of them improved, valued at $2,250, 4 horses, 5 milk cows, 7 cattle, 20 sheep, and 30 swine. In 1836, he was a partner in the Eagle Gold Mine.

- **Walker, Thomas**: 1870 tax records show that he owned 340 acres, 100 of them improved, valued at $3,050, 2 horses, 3 milk cows, 2 cattle, and 3 swine.

- **Weedon, John**: b. 1832? Purchased 130 acres from Ann Walker in 1856 for $1,300.50. The land is on the north side of Route 610, on the west side of Hazel Run. (DB 13-74); (*Enlisted in Company E, 7th Virginia Infantry*)

- **Wren, Philip**: Sketch showing the Operations of the Army of the Potomac locates a Wren property on the south side Route of 610, about two miles west of the fire tower. 1870 tax records show that he owned 137 acres, 72 of them improved, valued st $822, 2 horses, 3 milk cows, and 4 swine.

Appendix VIII

Postmasters

(National Archives and Records Service, Washington DC)

The post office at Richardsville was first at Smith's Tavern on December 15, 1828. The name was change to Richardsville on March 8, 1831. The of ficewas discontinued on September 29, 1866 and reestablished on March 11, 1868. Names of the postmasters are as follows:

- John Gathright; December 15, 1828
- William T. J. Richards; January 14, 1831
- William Rixey; January 1, 1835
- Charles C. Bailey; October 12, 1835
- James E. Chancellor; January 5, 1846
- Charles C. Bailey; January 20, 1846
- John B. Humphreys; December 23, 1847
- James W. Smith; January 20, 1852
- Flodorado H. Humphreys; January 7, 1853
- Samuel Walker; April 6/16?, 1858
- Johnson Smith; September 24, 1858
- Mary J. Foster; March 11, 1868
- Mrs. E. B. Walker; March 6, 1871
- Warrenton D. Foster; January 22, 1873
- Richard Lewis; April 10, 1874
- William C. Jameson; September 9, 1889
- James B. Rogers; May 27, 1889
- Joesph R. Fields; October 18, 1889
- Clover G. Dowdy; May 2, 1913
- Annie M. Allison; September 2, 1919
- Agnes F. Beach (Acting); January 1, 1942
- Frederick W. Taylor; January 23, 1942
- Mary Crosman (Acting); October 1, 1947
- Mrs. Thorne C. Lachine; April 27, 1949
- Catherine Feagan; November 30, 1950

Contract Number 1948: Wilderness via Chancellorsville, Richardsville and Stevensburg to Culpeper Court House. Twenty six miles let for the period 1839 to 1834 to I. N. C. Stockton of Charlottesville.
Contract Number 1811: From Fredericksburg via Richardsville and Stevensburg to Culpeper Court House. Thirty four miles let for the period 1839 to 1843 to George Johnson.
Contract Number 2413: From Fredericksburg via Chancellorsville, Richardsville and Stevensburg to Culpeper court House. Thirty seven miles the period 1843 to I and A Perkins.

Appendix IX,
GPS/MAP Coordinates (USNG/MGRS)

- Rogers Ford - 18S TH 6100 5556
- Ellis Ford - 18S TH 6469 5653
- Upper Ford - 18S TH 67265570
- Skinkers/Martins - 18S TH 6755 5565
- Pembertons Ford - 18S TH 6769 5559
- Bells Ford – 18S TH 6880 5491
- 0ld Emburys Ford 18S Th 7019 5265
- Richards Ford – 18S TH 7105 5137
- Blind Ford – 18S TH 6961 4897
- Todds Ford – 18S TH 6922 4905
- Hardins Ford – 18S TH 6952 5026
- Billingsby Ford – 18S TH 6804 5083
- Elys ford – 18S TH 6532 4913
- Emberys Ford – 18S TH 6349 4857
- Culpeper Mine/McNeils Ford – 18S TH 6271 5027
- Halls Ford – 18S TH 6046 51`23
- Skinkers Ford (Rapidan River) – 18S TH 6001 5206
- Humphreys/Weedonsd Ford 18S TH 5839 5294

BIBLIOGRAPHY

- Beaudry, Louis N., Records of the Fifth New York Cavalry, Albany, 1874.
- Boatner, Mark M. III, *The Civil War Dictionary*, New York, David McKay Company, Inc., 1959.
- Bushnell, David I. Jr., *The Manahoac Tribes In Virginia, 1608*, Smithsonian Institution, City of Washington, 1936.
- City of Fredericksburg, Virginia, *Historic Resources Along the Rappahannock and Rapidan Rivers.* Fredericksburg VA. Billingley Printing and Engraving, 2002.
- Coates, Earl J. and Thomas, Dean S., *An Introduction To Civil War Small Arms*, Gettysburg, PA, Thomas Publications, 1990.
- Collins, George K., *Memoirs of the 149th Regiment, New York Volunteer Infantry*, Syracuse, 1891.
- Couty, John, *Rappahannock River Canal Improvements*, 1845, Museum of Culpeper History, Culpeper VA.
- Culpeper County Deed Records, Clerks Office, Culpeper VA.
- Culpeper County Will Books, Clerks Office, Culpeper VA.
- Garnett, Carroll M., *Fort Lowry and Raiders on the Rappahannock*, New York, Vantage Press, 2002.
- Goolrick, William K., ed. Time-Life, *Rebels Resurgent*, Alexandria, Virginia, Time-Life Books, 1985.
- Editors of Time-Life Books, *Lee Takes Command*, Alexandria, Virginia, Time-Life Books, 1984.
- Editors of Time-Life Books, *Echoes of Glory, Illustrated Atlas of the Civil War*, Alexandria, Virginia, Time-Life Books, 1991.
- Fauquier Bicentennial Committee, *Fauquier County 1759 - 1959*, Warrington, VA, VA Publishing, 1959.
- Fauquier County Will Book, Fauquier Library, Warrenton VA.
- Fisher, Herbert G., "*The Virginia Piedmont- A Definition: A Review of the Physiological Attributes and Historic Land Use of This Region*", Piedmont Archaeology, Recent Research and Results, Archeological Society of America, Special Publication No. 10, 1983.
- Friends of the Rappahannock, *Rappahannock River Trail Guide*, 2006.
- Hilles, L. B., *Chickens Come Home to Roost*, New York, Mutual Publishing Co., 1899.
- Hodge, Robert, *1810 Culpeper County Census*, Culpeper Library, Culpeper VA, 1973.
- Jaynes, Gregory, *The Killing Ground*, Alexandria, Virginia, Time-Life Books, 1986.
- Jones, Mary Stevens, *An 18th Century Perspective: Culpeper County*,

Culpeper Historical Society, Inc., 1976.
- McNamara, D. George, *The History of the 9th Regiment Massachusetts Volunteer Infantry*, Boston, 1899.
- Moffett, Lee, *Water Powered Mills of Fauquier County, Virginia*, Fauquier County Public Library, 1974.
- National Archives and Records Service, *List of Postmasters, Richardsville Virginia*, Washington DC.
- New York Monuments Commission, *New York At Gettysburg, Vol. 2*, Albany, J. B. Lyon Company, 1900.
- Riggs, David F., *7th Virginia Infantry*, Lynchburg, Virginia, H. E. Howard, Inc., 1982.
- Riggs, David F., *13th Virginia Infantry*, Lynchburg, Virginia, H. E. Howard, Inc., 1988.
- Rights, Douglas L. and Cumming, William P., *The Discoveries of John Lederer*, Charlottesville, Virginia, University of Virginia Press, 1958.
- Rosenblatt, Emil and Ruth, *Hard Marching Every Day, The Civil War Letters of Private Wilbur Fisk, 1861 - 1865*, Lawrence, Kansas, University Press of Kansas, 1992.
- Scheel, Eugene M., *Culpeper, A Virginia County's History Through 1920*, Orange, Green Publishers, Inc., 1982.
- Scheel, Eugene M., *The Historical Site Survey and Archaeological Reconnaissance of Culpeper County, Virginia, November 1992 - April 1994*, Culpeper Library, Culpeper VA.
- Smith, John, ed. Edward Arber II , *The Generall Historie of Virginia,... in Travels and Works of Captain John Smith*, Edinburgh: John Grant, 1910.
- Smith, J. L., *History of the 118th Pennsylvania Volunteers*, Philadelphia, 1905.
- Steuert, Bradley W., *1870 Tax Records of Culpeper County*, Bountiful, Utah, Precision Printing, 1989.
- Sutherland, Daniel E., *Seasons of War,* New York, NY, The Free Press. 1995.
- Tobie, Edward P., *History of the First Maine Cavalry, 1861-1865*, Boston, 1887.
- *United States War Department, War of the Rebellion*: A Compilation of Official Records of the Union and Confederate Armies. Washington D.C. Government Printing Office, 1891- 895.
- 1850 Tax Records of Richardsville, Virginia State Library, Richmond VA.
- 1860 Tax Records of Richardsville, Virginia State Library, Richmond VA.
- 1870 Tax Records of Richardsville, Virginia State Library, Richmond VA.
- 1880 Tax Records of Richardsville, Virginia State Library, Richmond VA.

NEWSPAPERS

- Philadelphia Weekly Times.
- Culpeper Exponent.
- Culpeper Star Exponent.
- Town and Country, Free Lance-Star.

MAPS

- *1737 Lord Fairfax Survey of Northern Neck, Virginia*, Central Rappahannock Regional Library, Fredericksburg, VA.
- Baldwin, Laozi, State Engineer, *1817 Map of Rappahannock River*, Central Rappahannock Regional Library, Fredericksburg, VA.
- Campbell, A. H, Captain Provisional Engineers and Lieutenant Dwight, Chief of Topl. Dept, C.S.P. E., *Survey of Culpeper and Madison Counties, Virginia*, Library of Congress,1863.
- Couty, John, *Rappahannock River Canal Improvements, 1845*, Museum of Culpeper History, Culpeper VA.
- Hoffman, J. Paul, *Map of Orange County, Operations of Confederate and Union Forces*, by order Lt. Col. W. P. Smith, Central Rappahannock Regional Library, Fredericksburg, VA.
- Garden, H. D., *Map of Culpeper County, Va., 1876*, Museum of Culpeper History, Culpeper VA.
- Gilmer Colonel, *1863 Map of Culpeper County*, Museum of Culpeper History, Culpeper VA.
- Koerber, Captain V. E. von, *Picket Line of the First and Third Cavalry Divisions, Cavalry Corps, Army of the Potomac*, The Official Military Atlas of the Civil War, Washington, Government Printing Office, 1891-1895.
- *Map of Central Virginia Grants Campaign 1864 - 1865*, Marching Notes, prepared for Sec. Of War, Central Rappahannock Regional Library, Fredericksburg, VA.
- *1890's Map of the Powhatan Mining Company*.
- Map of Fauquier County, Central Rappahannock Regional Library, Fredericksburg, VA, No. 9, HR 817.
- *Map and Profile of the Rappahannock River and its Improvement, 1848*, Virginia State Library, MSS 755.2 H9 1848.
- McCary, Ben C., *John Smith's Map of Virginia*, Williamsburg, Virginia, Virginia 350th Anniversary Celebration Corp., 1963.
- Paine, Capt. W. H., A. D. C., *Map of part of Rappahannock River above*

Fredericksburg and the Rapid Ann River and the adjacent country, Complied under the direction of Col. J. N Macomb, A. D. C., Major Topi. Engrs., Library of Congress, December 1862.
- *Sketch showing the Operations or the Army of The Potomac, from Nov. 26 to Dec. 3, 1863*, The Official Military Atlas of the Civil War, Washington, Government Printing Office, 1891-1895.
- Schedler, J. engr., *Map of Culpeper County with parts of Madison, Rappahannock, and Fauquier Counties, Virginia*, Library of Congress.
- Scheel, Eugene M., *Map of Culpeper County,* drawn for the Second National Bank of Culpeper, Washington D. C., William and Heintz, 1975.
- Scheel, Eugene M., *1776 Map of Culpeper County,* drawn for the Second National Bank of Fauquier County, 1996.
- *The Official Military Atlas of the Civil War*, Washington, Government Printing Office, 1891-1895.
- Trout, W. E., *The Rappahannock Scenic River Atlas*, Virginia Canals and Navigation Society, 1992, U. S.
Geological Survey, Topographical Map, Wilderness Quadrangle, 1963.
- U. S. Geological Survey, Topographical Map, Richardsville Quadrangle, 1978.

INTERVIEWS

- Interview with Jim Beard, descendant of John Beard and Margaret Childs.
- Interview with Carl Douglas Green, descendent of Britton Green and Ida Hall.
- Interview Fred Ricker, Richardsville resident and Lewis Ellis descendant.

MANUSCRIPTS / JOURNALS

- Article of Margaret Johnson Martin.
- Brochure for *The Johnson Land Company*.
- Culpeper Connections, Journal of the Culpeper Genealogical Society, *Will of William Richards*, November 2003, Vol. 3, No. 2.
- Fred Ricker, Article on *Rappahannock City*, Richardsville VA.
- Letters of Morris Bartlett, Co. H, 102 NY Infantry.

ONLINE

- *"Civil War Map Collection,"* Map. Library of Congress, <http://memory.loc.gov/ammem/collections/civil_war_maps/>
- *Civil War Soldiers and Sailors System,* <http://www.itd.nps.gov/cwss/index.hml>
- Culpeper County, Virginia GIS, <http://www.onlinrgis.net/VaCulpeper/>
- Koplend Geneology, <http//home.swbell.net/Koplend>
- Hotchkiss, Jed, *A Map of Fauquier Co, Virginia,* Library of Congress, <http://memory.loc.gov/ammem/collections/civil_war_maps/>
- Hotchkiss, Jed, Library of Congress, *Report of the camps & engagements, of the Second Corps, A.N.V., and of the Army 0f the Valley Dist. of the Department of Northern VA, during the campaign of 1864: illustrated by maps & sketches by Jed Hotchkiss, No.1 and No.1a.: Battle of Wilderness and Spotsylvania Court House,* Library of Congress, <http://memory.loc.gov/ammem/collections/civil_war_maps/>
- Robinson, S. B., *The Battle of Chancellorsville Sunday, May 3rd, 1863* Library of Congress, <http://memory.loc.gov/ammem/collections/civil_war_maps/>
- Paine, Capt. W. H., A. D. C. *Map of a part of the Rappahannock River above Fredericksburg and the Rapid Ann River and the adjacent country,* Library of Congress, December 1862, <http://memory.loc.gov/ammem/collections/civil_war_maps/>
- The Early Discoveries of John Lederer, 1644, Map, <http://www.alexanderstreet2.com/EENALive/bios/A6812BI.html>

INDEX

Symbols
8th Pennsylvania Cavalry 13, 39, 41

A
Adams Branch 31
African American School 78
Algonkian 3, 4
Allcock 13
Allen's Dam 49, 84
Allen, Thomas 84
Allison, Annie M. 123
Allison, Robert 103, 121
Allison, T. L. 101
Amoroleck 4, 5, 6
Armistead's Mill 72
Ashby, William Aylett 84
Averell, Brigadier General William 11

B
Bailey, Charles 101
Bailey's Tavern 79, 80
Baldwin, Laozi 30, 49
Ball's/ Garthright's Tavern 79
Barnes, Colonel James 12
Barnett, Benjamin Jr. 30
Barnett, Benjamin Sr. 30
Barnett, Isabella 30
Barnett, Richard 33
Barnetts Ford 37, 42, 98, 101
Barnett's Mill 30, 31, 48, 72, 76, 121
Bauder, Ezra 36
Bauder, Julia 36, 101
Beach, Agnes F. 123
Beach, Evans 79
Beach family 115
Beach Road 18, 78, 79, 81, 82, 85, 86, 102, 104
Beach's Store 79, 115
Beard, John 128
Bell Cemetery 20
Bell Farm 19
Bell, George W. 84, 102
Bell, Richard 102
Bells Ford iii, 18, 19, 25, 84, 85, 102, 124
Bells Ford Road 18
Bell's house 18, 82
Bell, William T. 102

Benedict 26
Benson, Dulcibel C. (Richards) 118
Benson, Winfred Berry (Richards) 119
Berdan sharpshooters 12
Billingsby Ford 70, 124
Blakeslee, Major Erastus 100
Blind Ford 25, 70, 71, 124
Boals, James 114
Bower's Blacksmith Shop: 81
Bradshaw, Mrs. 102
Brandy Rifles 84, 88
Brandy Station 15, 36, 41, 44, 45, 86, 87, 88, 91, 97, 101
Brandy Station Secondary School 101
Brandy Station Wheatley Academy 36
Brinkerhoff, Isabella 32
Brinkerhoff, Lewis 32
Brinton, Lt. Col. William P. 100
Brodhead, Colonel 38, 39
Brooke, John L. 85
Brook sisters 110
Brown, Francis J. 85
Brown, Mr. (Culpepper) 79
Brown, Thomas 22
Bryan, Col. Timothy M. Jr. 100
Buford, Brigadier General 38
Bullard, Anne 27
Burke, Basal 52
Burnside, Major General 38
Burton's Cemetery 82
Burton, Thomas 85
Burton, William P. 85
Bushnell, David I. 125
Butzner 35

C
Capeheart, Major Charles E. 100
Catlett, John 6
Cavalry Division, 3rd 15, 97, 99
Cesnola, Colonel Di 11, 13
Chancellor, James C. 103
"Chickens Come Home to Roost" 17, 125
Childs 102
Childsburg Mine 74
Childs, Emma 102
Childs, Francis 102
Childs, George 102

Childs (Hall), Mary 102
Childs (Humphreys), Susan Jane 110
Childs, Margaret 102, 128
Childs, W. 103
City Field 37
Coffee, P. J. 85
Colbert, A. L. 103
Colbert's Cemetery 82
Cole, F. M. 85
Cole, J. C. 85
Coleman cemetery 85, 86
Coleman, Robert M. 85
Coleman, Wilson A. 86
Cole's Store 80
Company E, 13th VA Infantry 106
Connecticut, 1st Cavalry 99
Coppage, R. E. 103
Coppage's Store 79
Couty, John 8, 9, 21, 23, 31, 33, 50
Crawley's Dam 18
Crawley's Mill 19
Cromarty Mine 74, 78
Crosman, Mary 123
Culpeper Gold Mine 75, 114
Culpeper Mine 15, 70, 71, 72, 74, 96, 97, 98, 102, 124
Culpeper Mine Ford 15, 70, 71, 96, 97, 98
Culpeper Mine Mill 72
Culpeper Mining Company 71, 74
Culpeper Riflemen 84, 88, 91
Curtis, Douglas 103
Curtis, Frank 103
Curtis (Hall), Nancy 107
Curtis, Jesse 86, 103
Curtis, Jim 103
Curtis, John F. 103
Curtis Mill Road 79, 102, 111, 112
Curtis, Susan 104
Curtis, Thomas O. 86
Curtis, W. 104
Curtis, Walter S. 86
Curtis, William 112
Custer, Brigadier General 14

D
Daverson, Lillie 104
Davies, (Colonel) Brigadier General Henry 16, 25, 45, 51
Deep Run 19, 22

Devin, Colonel Thomas 38, 42
Downey, Darby 86
Downing, Captain 15
Dry Bottom Mine 75
Duffie, Colonel 39, 51
Dunn, Helen 34
Dunn, John 34

E
Eagle Gold Mine 122
Eagle Mining Company 74
Eley, Carl 25, 26, 118
Eley, Edward 25, 26
Eley's Ford 45
Eley's/Quarles' Mill 72
Ellington, John 86, 104
Ellington, Virginia 86, 104
Ellis Ferry 31
Ellis Ford iii, 11, 12, 16, 24, 29, 33, 34, 37, 38, 39, 40, 41, 42, 43, 44, 45, 46, 48, 49, 60, 63, 72, 74, 75, 76, 77, 87, 97, 98, 99, 101, 104, 109, 112, 114, 119, 121, 122, 124
Ellis Ford Road 74, 75, 77, 109
Ellis Gold Mining and Reduction Company 34
Ellis, Lewis 31, 32, 33, 34, 37, 48, 74, 75, 76, 109, 114, 128
Ellis Mine 34, 53, 75, 78, 81
Ellis Mine Hunt Club Road 78
Ellis's house 33
Ellis's Mill 37, 72
Embrey, Eddie 105
Embrey, Fred 112
Embrey, H. A. 31
Embrey, Hezekiah 32
Embrey, Joseph 76
Embrey Mine 76, 105
Embreys Ford 70
Embrey's Mill 32
Enterprise Mine (Eagle) 75

F
Fallis's Mill 30
Farabee, Major Harvey 100
Feagan, Catherine 123
Federal Land Bank of Baltimore 50
Field, Daniel 87, 105
Field, Henry 105
Field, James R. 105

Field, Joesph R. 105
Field, Lucy Ann 106
Field's Cemetery 82
Fields Ford 114
Field's Mill 72, 105
Fields Mill Road 72, 82, 85, 86, 87
Field, Thomas 106
Field, W. H. 106
Field, William D. 106
Fifth Corps, 1st Division 12, 14, 40
Fifth Corps, 2nd Division 14
First Cavalry Division 41
Fisk, Wilbur 46, 47, 126
Fitzhugh, Captain 10
Foster, Frank 80
Foster, Mary J. 106, 123
Foster's Store 80, 103
Foster, W. D. 36, 80, 110
Franklin Mines 110
Fredericksburg, Battle of 19, 24, 27, 39, 50, 89
Fredericksburg Power Company 32
Fredericksburg property 22
Fredericksburg Virginia Herald 31
Free Meeting House 81

G
Garret, Richard 36
Garthright's Tavern 79
Gatewood, Martha 106
Gathright, John 123
Geary, Brigadier General Jonathan 24, 51, 96
Germanna Ford 15
German Savings and Loan 35, 76
Gills Run 78, 81
Glosler 22
Gold Mines iii, 23, 33, 74, 75, 76, 104, 105, 112, 114
Goldvein 21, 22, 23, 28
Greeley Mine 75
Green, Britton 72, 128
Greene, General George 24, 42, 51
Gregg, Brigadier General 44, 45
Greggs Cavalry Division 96
Griffin, Brigadier General 38
Griffin's brigade 38
Grims, C. 107
Grimsley, Richard T. 87
Grove Church 23, 97

Grove Meeting House 30
Groves, Joseph R. 87

H
Hackley 31
Hall, Alexander 82, 102, 107, 108
Hall, Amy 107
Hall, Bradley 80, 107, 108, 113, 120
Hall cemetery 82, 108
Hall, Charles 107
Hall, Daniel 82, 104, 107
Hall, Dr. Arthur 107, 120
Hall family 71
Hall farm (Mastin Property) 82
Hall (Green), Ida 107, 128
Hall, Lula Davis 105, 108
Hall, Mattie Larkin 108
Hall Mine 76
Hall, O. G. 108
Hall, Philip 108
Hall, Sanford F. 108, 120
Halls Ford 71, 107, 108, 124
Halls Road 78, 82, 107
Hall, Virginia (Weedon) 82
Hall, William 108
Hammond, Major John 100
Hansbrough, William L. 87
Harding house 115
Harding, Richard 108
Hardins Ford 70, 108, 124
Hardin's Mill 72, 78, 108
Harris, Judith 110
Hartwood Church 11, 13, 15, 37, 39
Hassiningua 3
Hawkins, Ned 16
Hazel Run 72, 78, 81, 103, 107, 108, 117, 122
Heflin, John L. 87
Hickerson, J. 108
Hickerson, W. 109
Hilles, L. B. 17, 125
Hooker, General Joseph 11, 12, 13, 40
Hoopers Branch 82
Horace Greeley Mine 75
Horseshoe 16, 53
Humphreys, Ann M. 7, 109, 119
Humphreys, Bettie Lewis 109
Humphreys, Captain Andrew Jackson 109
Humphreys, Captain (Colonel) Thomas 111

Humphreys, Catherine A 109
Humphrey's Cemetery 82
Humphrey's estate 26, 28, 110
Humphreys, Flodoardo 28, 82
Humphreys Ford 71
Humphreys, James Richards 110
Humphreys, Jeff 110
Humphreys, John B. 110
Humphreys, Judith 28
Humphreys, Lewis E. 87
Humphreys, Lucy 110
Humphreys, Malvina 111
Humphreys (Pemberton), Isabella Miller 110
Humphreys (Richard), Elizabeth 8
Humphreys, Rufus J. 88
Humphreys, Sarah 27
Humphreys, S. E. 111
Humphreys, Thomas Jefferson 111
Humphreys, William Thomas 111
Hunt, Cumberland A. 88

J
Jacobs Ford 96
Jameson, William C. 123
Jennings, Edward 88
Jennings Farm 97
Jennings, George (Tom) 111
Jennings, Joseph 112
Jennings Road 86, 101, 103, 104
Jennings Run 73
Jennings shop 111
Jennings's Mill 73
Jennings, Susan 112
Jerrys Flats 70
Johnson, Anna 35
Johnson, Captain 39
Johnson Creek 35
Johnson Gold Mine 23
Johnson Land Company 35, 128
Johnson Land Company, The 35, 128
Johnson, Larman G. 34, 35, 36, 76, 112
Johnson, Margaret 35, 128
Johnson, M. L. 32
Johnson's Cemetery 82
Johnson's Mine 23
Jones, Harry 79
Jones, J and C 112
Jones, John R. 112
Jones, Lucretia 111

Jones, Roy 112
Jones, William 88, 112, 113
Jones, William T. 88, 113
Jordon, Henry 99

K
Kelly Mine 34
Kellys Ford 10, 11, 13, 14, 25, 29, 38, 39, 40, 43, 44, 51
Kelly's mill 23
Kemper, Charlotte 27
Kemper, Colonel W. S. 27
Kemper, George 52
Kemper, Henry N. 113
Kemper, James Lawson 27
Kemper, M. J. 113
Kempers dam 45
Kempers Ford iii, 42, 49, 50, 51
Kemper's house 51
Kemper, William 113
Kent, Letta 34
Kent, Linden 34
Kent, Robert 34
Kilpatrick, Brigadier General 44
King, D. L. 34
Kite, James H. 88

L
Lachine, Mrs. Thomas C. 123
Lawrence, S. D. 99
Leary, Gordon and Patricia 52
Lederer, John 5, 6, 49, 126, 129
Lewis, George 88
Lewis, Richard 123
Liberty Mines 110
Lick Run 72, 107
Lignum 78, 84, 86
Locust Hill 8, 50, 71, 72, 82, 88, 103, 107, 111, 113
Lord Fairfax 7, 30, 72, 127
Love, Almeda 113
Love Mine 76
Love, W. B. 113
Lucas, Albert G. 75
Luckett, Samuel R. 88

M
Maddens Tavern 78
Madden, T. O. 78

Maine, 1st cavalry 45, 97
Maine, 6th Volunteers 13
Mannahannock Park 35
Marean, Harold S. 113
Marean, H. S. 103
Marganna 35, 62, 63, 64, 66, 74, 76, 104
Marganna Mine 62, 64, 76
Marganna Mining Company 35
Marganna, West 35, 74, 76, 104
Martin, Archie 79
Martin, John S. 89
Martin, L. W. 113
Martin, Martha 114
Martin, Murry "Buck" 28, 114
Martin, Pete 114
Martin, Robert 114
Martin, Sanford 114
Martin's battery 14
Martin's farm 21, 27, 28, 114
Martin, William 81
Massachusetts, 9th Volunteer Infantry 37
Mastin, Francis 79
Mastin, James 114
Mastin property 82
Maupin, Ella 17, 82
Maupin, Horace 28, 82, 115, 117
Maupin, Minnie 82
Maupin's Cemetery 82
McChonchie, Marvin, P 115
McConchie, James H. 88
McConchie, John W. 115
McMurran, Joseph 89
McNeils Ford 70, 71, 124
McNeil's house 71
Melville Mines 70
Merritt, Lieutenant 98
Michigan, 1st Cavalry 38, 96
Middle Run 76, 103
Mill Bank 31, 32, 33, 74, 75, 76
Mill Bank Mines 33, 76
Mill Bank Mining company 74
Millburn 22
Miller, B. D. 115
Miller, Eliza 119
Miller, Simon 115
Miller's Mill 73–141, 115–141
Miller's Store 80
Miller, W. H. 115
Mill Run 72, 82, 105

Mills, David 17
Mine Run Campaign 15, 44, 45, 51, 96, 97, 99
Mitchell, John W. 75
Mitchell, William W. 75
Mohaskahod 4, 6
Morrel, Major General 38
Morrel's Division 38
Morrisville 11, 12, 15, 44, 45, 47, 51
Mortons Ford 98
Mosco 4
Mountain Run 50, 89, 91
Mt. Ephraim 22
Mt. Ephraims Road 18
Munson, Lieutenant 46
Murphy, Eddie 79

N

Neck, The 1, 49, 50, 74, 115, 119
Newby, E. A. 115
Newby, Henry 115
Newby, Major William P. 26
Newby, Mary 115
Newby, R. C. 115
Newcomer, Emanuel 89
New York, 2nd Cavalry 97, 100
New York, 5th Cavalry 24, 25
New York, 6th Cavalry 38, 40, 43
New York, 8th Cavalry 15
New York, 10th Cavalry 47, 48
New York, 102nd Infantry 42
New York, 137th Infantry 51
New York, 146th Infantry 14
New York, 149th Infantry 24
North Carolina, 63rd Cavalry 41

O

Oakland Baptist Church 1, 8, 28, 79, 81, 90, 105, 110, 115, 120, 121
Oakland Baptist Church Cemetery 28, 81
Oak Shade 21, 26, 28, 32, 53, 82, 110, 116, 117
Old Pine School 78, 81
Orchard Farm 26, 66, 72, 74, 78, 81, 82, 105, 109, 113, 115, 116
Orchard Farm Cemetery 82
Orchard Farm Church 72, 81
Orchard Farm School, First 78
Orchard Farm School, Second 78

P

Parnell, Captain 40
Peach Grove 21, 22, 27, 28, 115, 117
Peachwood 102, 117
Pemberton, Ann Bullard 83
Pemberton, Bettie 116
Pemberton, Catherine (Kitty) 116
Pemberton Cemetery 82, 116
Pemberton, Eliza 27, 32, 65, 114, 116
Pemberton (Humphreys), Isabella 110, 116
Pemberton, J. O. 116
Pemberton, John 116
Pemberton, Larkin 116
Pemberton, Lucy 117
Pemberton, Malvina S. 117
Pemberton, Mary A. 116
Pemberton (Maupin), Minnie 117
Pemberton, Oswald N. 117
Pemberton, Sarah (Sallie) F. 117
Pemberton's Cemetery, Oak Shade 82
Pemberton's Cemetery, Orchard Farm 82
Pemberton's Shop 81
Pemberton's Slave Cemetery, Orchard Farm 82
Pemberton, Thomas L. 89, 117
Pemberton, William P. 89
Pennsylvania, 3rd Cavalry 12, 39
Pennsylvania, 18th Cavalry 16
Pennsylvania, 109th Volunteer Infantry 51
Pennsylvania, 111th Volunteer Infantry 51
Pennsylvania, 118th Volunteer Infantry 12, 126
Perkins, I and A 123
Pie Island 19
Pilgrims Church 71
Pine View 22, 29, 39
Pittsburg Company 35, 76
Pleasonton, Brigadier General Alfred 50
Point Comfort 118, 119
Pope, General 9, 24, 37
Powell, Elisha 9
Powell, Hugh Ptolemy 89
Powells Canal 9, 18
Powhatan Mining Company 34, 35, 36, 76, 101, 112, 127
Preston, Lt. Col. 96
Publican Church 81
Pucketts 52

Purcell Lumber Company 34, 35

Q

Quarles' Mill 72

R

Rapidan River Fords iii, 70
Rappahannock City 34, 35, 36, 37, 48, 53, 74, 76, 101, 120, 122, 128
Rappahannock River Campground 28, 32, 114
Rappahannock River Canal Company 8, 21, 31, 33, 49, 50
Rappahannock River canal system 8, 9, 19, 21, 23
Rappahannock Station 10, 14, 15, 38, 41, 42, 44, 51
Rattle Snake Castle 30
Redd, Phillip D. 89
Red Front Store 80
Reynolds, Morton 118
Reynolds, Robert 118
Richards/Barnett's Cemetery 83
Richards, Benjamin Franklin 7, 118
Richards, Captain William 119
Richards Dam 9, 18
Richards, Elizabeth 118, 119
Richards, Eliza Lewis 7, 118
Richard's Ferry 8
Richards Ferry Road 16, 18
Richards Ford 3, 5, 6, 7, 8, 9, 10, 11, 12, 13, 14, 15, 16, 17, 18, 19, 21, 28, 40, 41, 50, 73, 83, 96, 115, 118, 119, 120, 121, 124
Richards, Harriet 7
Richards house 8, 12, 16, 17
Richards, Isabella 119
Richards, James 8, 73, 110, 118, 119
Richards, John J. 7, 119
Richards, John Royal 119
Richards, Kathy 118
Richards, Martha 12
Richards Mills 8
Richards, Mollie M. 7, 119
Richards, Samuel 119
Richards, Sarah 7
Richards Slave Cemetery 83
Richardsville i, iii, iv, 1, 6, 7, 8, 12, 13, 15, 16, 17, 18, 19, 20, 26, 27, 28, 31, 33, 37, 41, 45, 48, 65, 67, 78, 79, 80, 81,

83, 84, 85, 86, 87, 88, 89, 90, 91, 96, 97, 98, 99, 101, 102, 103, 105, 106, 107, 108, 110, 112, 114, 118, 119, 120, 123, 126, 128
Richardsville Country Store 78, 79, 80, 107
Richardsville Fire Department 79, 118
Richardsville Methodist Cemetery 102
Richardsville Methodist Church 16, 28, 97, 99, 106
Richardsville Post Office 79
Richardsville School, First 79
Richardsville School, Second 79
Richardsville School, Third 79
Richards, William 7, 8, 12, 16, 17, 20, 26, 27, 28, 30, 50, 101, 111, 115, 119, 121, 128
Richards, William Thomas Jefferson 119
Ricker's house 79, 80
River Beach Road 102
River Hill Farm 82, 108
Rixey, William 123
Rock Run 21, 22, 23, 24, 27, 68
Rocky Ford 21, 23
Rodgers, James F. 90, 120
Rodgers, John F. 89
Rodgers, Welford N. 120
Rodgers, Willie F. 50
Rogers Ford 49, 50, 51, 52, 84, 120, 124
Rogers Ford Winery 52
Roger's house 50
Rogers, James B. 80, 123
Roger's Store 80, 121
Rogers, Thomas 80
Rossin Mountain 76
Rosson Mine 76
Route 610 (Elys Ford Road) 49, 50, 72, 75, 78, 79, 80, 81, 82, 83, 85, 86, 98, 102, 103, 104, 105, 107, 108, 111, 112, 115, 117, 120, 121, 122
Route 619 (Richards Ferry Road) 18, 74, 77, 78, 80, 81, 83, 102, 109, 116, 118, 119, 122
Route 683 (River Mill Road) 28, 82, 110, 114, 115, 116
Route 703 (Walker Road) 81
Route 733 (Curtis Mill Road) 112
Route 743 (Beach Road) 18, 102, 104
Royall, John J. 30
Royal, Mr. 24

S

Salvation Army 35, 86, 104
Saxton Junction 11
Scott, J. Z. H. 46
Second Cavalry Division 15, 42, 45, 99
Shakahonea 4
Sheppard's Grove Post Office 45
Sisson, William T. 90
Skinker, Edward 19
Skinkers Canal 23
Skinkers Dam 24
Skinkers Ford 17, 19, 21, 22, 23, 24, 25, 26, 27, 32, 42, 43, 51, 68, 69, 71, 73, 80, 81, 82, 89, 96, 97, 102, 103, 105, 110, 111, 114, 115, 116, 117, 118, 121, 124
Skinker's Mill 22, 24, 73
Skinkers Mill, 1st 22
Skinkers Mill, 2nd (Spring Mill) 22
Skinkers Mill, 3rd 22
Skinker, S. T. 71
Skinker, Thomas 22
Skinker, William Jr. 22
Smith, Almeda 107
Smith, D. R. 90
Smith Farm 120, 121
Smith (Hall), Fonce 120
Smith (Hall), Laura 120
Smith, James W. 120
Smith, John Minor 120
Smith, John R. 90
Smith, Johnson 90, 120
Smith, Martin Vanburen 90
Smith's Tavern 1, 7, 90, 107, 120, 123
Smith Tract Gold Mine 76
Smith, William K. 31
Snake Castle Dam 35
Snake Castle Rock 32, 33
Sons of America Patriotic Club 78
Southard, H. 121
Southards Crossing 98
South Carolina, 1st Cavalry 12, 15
Spilman, Mason 16
Spring Hill 22
Spring Mill 22
Starkey, Lucy A. 121
Staunton- Barnett house 48
Staunton's Mill 30, 72, 121

Staunton, William 30, 72, 121
Stegora 4
Stevens, Brigadier General 38
Steven's Division 38
Stockton, I. N. C. 123
Strother, J. C. 121
Strother, Philip 90
Sulphur Springs 10, 38
Susquehannock 5
Suthard, John F. 90
Suthard, William T. 91

T
Talbot, Sir William 6
Taliaferro, Robert 6
Tauxuntania 4
Tayler, J. J. 121
Taylor, Frederick W. 123
Third Brigade, 2nd Division, 12th Corps 24
Thomas, Major 25
Thomas, P. L. 121
Thorn, Bill 25, 26
Thorn, William 121
Timberlake, Ben 17
Timberlake, Ella Maupin 17, 82
Timberlake Gold Mine 76
Timberlake, John 17, 28
Timberlake, Melissa 17
Timberlake, Rosser 26
Todds Ford 70, 118, 124
Todds Ford Road 118
Turner, T. R. 121
Turner, Zacharia R. 121
Tyson, Joseph 91

U
Union Baptist Church 81
Union Gold Mine 23
United States Mine Ford 11, 24
Urquhart, Charles 36, 101
Urquhart, John P. 77
Urquhart, Louisa 36
Urquhart Mine 34, 77
Urquhart, Samuel 34
Urquhart's Mill 73
Utz, Elizabeth 107

V
Vanaukin 80

Van Vorhis, Major Harvey B. 100
Vermont, 1st Cavalry 14, 96
Virginia, 9th Cavalry 15
Virginia, 17th Infantry 109
Virginia Gold Mining Company 75
Virginia Infantry, 13th, Company E 17, 20, 27, 28, 76, 102, 103, 104, 105, 109, 111, 113, 118, 120, 121
Virginia Militia, 5th Regiment 106
Voegthy, Edwin 20

W
Walker, Alexander D. 91
Walker, Ann 122
Walker, Burruss 26, 35, 122
Walker farm 83
Walker, J. 122
Walker, John S. 91
Walker, J. T. 122
Walker, Mrs. E. B. 123
Walker, Myrtle 118
Walker Road 80, 81, 83, 122
Walker, Samuel 122
Walker's Slave Cemetery 83
Walker's Store 80
Walker, Thomas 122
Wallis ford 38
Watson Ford 19
Waugh Run 114
Weedon, Isaac 108
Weedon, John 103, 108, 122
Weedon's farm 79, 103
Weedons Ford 71
Weedon, Virginia Hall 82
West, Edward 8
Wharton, Staunton 91
Wheatley Academy 36, 101
Wheatley, Behethelon 116
White, Major Amos H. 100
White Rock Road 87, 105
Whites Chapel 83
Whites Chapel Cemetery 83
Wilderness Run 70, 72
Williams, Thomas 34, 35
Wood, Silas 74
Woodville, Robert E. 91
Wren, Philip 122
Wycoff Mine

CPSIA information can be obtained at www.ICGtesting.com
Printed in the USA
BVIW12n0312211015
423435BV00002B/3